Scotch & Wry

Scotch & Wry

Starring

Rikki Fulton

Edited by Gordon Menzies

By arrangement with the
British Broadcasting Corporation.

Photographs by Tom Howat

GORDON WRIGHT PUBLISHING
25 MAYFIELD ROAD, EDINBURGH EH9 2NQ
SCOTLAND

British Library Cataloguing in Publication Data

Fulton, Rikki
Scotch & Wry.
1. Scottish wit and humor
1. Title 11. Menzies, Gordon
791.45'7 PN1992.77.S3/

ISBN 0-903065-56-8

Typeset by Gordon Wright Publishing.
Printed and bound by Billing & Sons Ltd., Worcester.

Contents

Foreword

When two million people in Scotland switch on their television sets on Hogmanay to watch a comedy programme it throws an awesome responsibility on the perpetrators. *Scotch & Wry* began in 1978 and we have been fortunate in keeping together the same production team, many of the writers and the four main performers, Gregor Fisher, Claire Nielson, Tony Roper and the incomparable Rikki Fulton.

I first worked with Rikki on an earlier programme I produced called *The Scotched Earth Show*. During rehearsals he had the tears running down my cheeks and our partnership was born. Without doubt Rikki is a brilliant comedy actor as distinct from being a stand-up comedian (although he can hold his own in that area too). His realisation of many of the characters created by script-writers literally lifts the words off the page into memorable television sketches. His timing is admired and envied by his fellow-performers. And, of course, as several of the following scripts indicate, Rikki Fulton is a writer in his own right.

Scotch & Wry was also fortunate in that it filled a gap. The writers and the performers were available but no-one was making Scottish comedy programmes for television. Metropolitan humour was widely available but the distinctively Scottish voice was not being heard.

Scotch & Wry, like comedy sketch shows everywhere, finds much of its material in the quirks and peculiarities of human behaviour. But the essence of *Scotch & Wry* humour is in its distinctive Scottish performance and language. There are no kilts or bagpipes or folk-singers in *Scotch & Wry* except as targets for the writers' arrows. The series has no truck with crookit bawbees, buts and bens and jokes about flying haggises. If heather-tinted myths do rear their ugly heads you can be sure that those heads will be cut off.

Some of the characters that have been created for Rikki have helped to make *Scotch & Wry* an annual cult on Hogmanay. The glaikit traffic policeman known as Supercop keeps failing to make that crucial arrest. And the Last Calls of the men of the cloth have literally persuaded some reverend gentlemen to refuse invitations to appear on the real thing. There is little doubt that the Rev. I.M. Jolly is better known and loved than many a religious eminence.

Television comedy is team-work. The performers and producers put flesh on the bones supplied by the writers. It is that unique combination of idea and performance, of gag and delivery, that enables *Scotch & Wry* to produce the sound of laughter in countless Scottish homes.

Gordon Menzies

The Magic of Christmas

by John Byrne

Woman: Rikki Fulton
Punk: Gregor Fisher
Santa: Tony Roper
Assistant: Judith Sweeney
Mother: Claire Nielson

In Santa's grotto at the end of a very busy and hectic Christmas Eve. Santa has just finished seeing what he imagines to be the last customer of the day.

Santa: Right, Timothy . . . now remember what Santa told you . . . You be a good boy now.

Mother: Oh, he will be good . . .

Santa: That's the stuff . . . bye, bye, now . . . and have a very merry Christmas. Bye, bye . . .

As Timothy and his mother leave, Santa heaves a sigh of relief, throws back his hood, hitches up his whiskers and slumps back into his chair. He pulls out a fag and lights up.
A female assistant pops her head round the door of the grotto.

Assistant: There's just one last customer, Mr. McKay. Do you want me to tell them you're shut?

Santa: No, no . . . that would never do . . . *(he nips his fag and sticks it behind his ear)* Just let me get my whiskers sorted and I'll be right with you . . . How's that? Right, on you go.

Assistant: Right madam, if you and your son would like to go in, Santa will see you now . . .

A woman in a headscarf enters. She is carrying two shopping bags. A fag hangs from her lip.

Woman: He's jist comin' Santa.

The woman turns and shouts back out through the door.

Woman: Will you hurry up an' no keep Santa waitin' Edward! *(she gives Santa a reassuring smile)* He's been waitin' fur over five 'oors tae see ye, Santa. Ye wull tell him he's gonnae huv a wonderful Christmas, wulln't ye?

Santa: Of course I will, madam . . .

Woman: He's the only wean left up oor close that still believes in ye . . . yu'll no dae nothin' tae . . .

Santa: Disillusion him? Certainly not . . . wouldn't dream of it. To me the magic of Christmas is a sacred trust . . .

Woman: Ooh that's lovely that. Edward! Get you in here!

A very reluctant punk enters. He is wearing a tattered leather jerkin covered in zips, straps, pins etc. He has a mohican haircut (yellow with red tips), tartan skintight drainpipes and big boots.

Santa: Good God!

Woman: Say hullo tae Santa. Say hullo tae Santa, Ah said.

She hits the punk a skite on the head.

Punk: Haw . . . chuck that!

Woman: Say hullo tae Santa, well!

Punk: *(aggressively)* Hullo, Santa!

Woman: Say hullo nice! *(she hits him again).*

Punk: Ahyah! *(even more aggressively)* Hullo, Santa!

Woman: That's better.

Santa: Er . . . hello . . . sonny.

Woman: Edward. His name's Edward . . . it's whit his faither an' me cry him . . . innit, stupit?

She hits him another skite across the side of his head.

Punk: Oucha!

Woman: Efter King Edward . . .

Santa: The eighth?

Woman: Naw, the tottie. He's a right eejit, so he is. Ah'm tellin' Santa yur a dumplin'

Punk: Ah'm ur nut a dumplin'

Woman: Ye widnae think tae luk at him he hud five highers, wid ye?

Santa: Good heavens . . . he's got five highers?

Woman: Naw, that's whit Ah'm sayin' . . . ye widnae think tae luk at him! Tell Santa whit ye want fur yur Christmas.

Punk: Ah want hur an' ma Da tae stoap smackin' us ower the napper . . . They keep smackin' us ower the napper . . .

Woman: Stoap tellin' Santa yur lies, d'ye hear! *(she smacks him over the head).*

Punk: Ahyah!

Woman: Tell him whit ye want fur yur Christmas . . . oan ye go . . . sit oan his knee an' tell Santa whit ye want fur yur Christmas! An' if you mention glue, Ah'll stick yur heid in this bag, so Ah wull! C'moan . . . up oan tae his knee . . .

Santa: No, no . . . if the lad doesn't want to sit on my knee then don't . . .

The punk is forced onto Santa's knee by his mother.

Woman: An' don't you dare vomit ower Santa's nice rid suit, Ah'm warnin' ye! *(she hits the punk another skite).*

Punk: Chuck it! Tell hur tae chuck it, Santa!

Woman: Speak up fur yersel' . . . tell Santa whit ye want. He wants somethin' special daen't ye!

Punk: Aye.

Santa: Fine . . . what . . . er . . .exactly . . . ?

Woman: Tell him . . . oan ye go . . . tell him! Stoap footerin' wi' that knife an' tell him!

Punk: *(mumbling)* Ah want a joab . . .

Woman: Tell him again . . . he's no gonnae bite ye!

Punk: Ah want a joab!

Woman: He wants a joab!

Santa: Er . . . well . . . that is interesting . . . yes . . .er . . .

Woman: He wants tae go an' work fur you . . . daen't ye, stupit!

Santa: For me?

Woman: Up at the North Pole . . .

Santa: Suffering God . . . *(he drops his head into his hands).*

Woman: He's oan the YTS the noo . . . uren't ye, Edward?

Punk: Aye . . .

Woman: Well, tell the man!

Punk: Tell him whit?

Woman: Tell him whit yur oan, glaikit!

Punk: Whit fur? Ah've already told the doacter . . .

Woman: No that, stupit appearance! Tell him how yur oan YTS an' ye want tae jine the reindeers an' the Seven Dwarfs up at the North Pole an' make toys oota chunksa wid an' spread joy an' happiness throughout the world an' Glesga every Christmas 'cos yur a good boy an' besides yur faither an' me'll be glad tae see the back o' ye! Tell him!

Santa: Look madam, I don't think you quite understand . . . you see, I'm not really in a position to . . .

Woman: Ur you here fur tae make every kiddie's Christmas Dream come true or ur ye not? That's whit the sign says ootside yur Grotto . . .

Santa: Yes, but . . .

Woman: Gie him a joab or yull be up afore the authorities fur contravenin' the Trades Descriptions Act . . .

Santa: Now, hold on here a minute . . .

Woman: Or if we don't get ye oan that wull huv ye up before the Race Relations Board! Whit's up . . . is it his height yur boathered aboot?

Santa: Height?

Woman: Is it because ye only employ gnomes, is that it? Well, let me tell you . . . *(turning to the punk)* stoap pickin' yur plooks, ya big eejit!

Santa: Look here, Madam, I've had a very busy day so if you could . . .

Woman: *(turning to go)* Mind an' gie us a phone when ye get there, Edward . . .

Punk: Right, Mammy . . .

Woman: He jist needs a hose doon wance a fortnight . . . get wanna yur elfs tae dae it. Cheerio, son . . .

Punk: Cheerio, Mammy . . . *(he turns to Santa and flicks his beard with his knife)* Dae ye want tae gie me ma first weeks wages now?

Woman: God, isn't it wonderful . . . the Magic of Christmas . . .

Hogmanay at the Police Station

by David Slade and Frank Walsh

Sergeant: Rikki Fulton
W.P.C.: Phyllis Logan

Inside a police station there is absolute chaos. Decorations hang amongst the debris. We see a clock on the wall. It is midnight. A few bodies lie around. Rioting is heard outside. A desk sergeant stands untouched by all this havoc.
A W.P.C. enters from the street - bedraggled - covered in blood and dust. She clambers over the debris.

W.P.C.: Quiet night this year, sarge!

Sergeant: *(mysteriously)* It's too quiet . . . that's what I'm afraid of.

The Rude Awakening

by Bernard Cranwell

Vet: Rikki Fulton
Woman: Claire Nielson

A vet is awakened from his sleep by his telephone ringing.

Vet: Er . . . hello . . . yes this is the Vet speaking . . . yes . . . yes whatever do you want at this time of the night! Don't you know it's two o'clock in the morning!

Woman: *(from a telephone box)* Sorry, but I need some urgent advice. Do you know how I can separate two dogs?

Vet: Yes, all you have to do is give them a ring on the telephone.

Woman: *(astonished)* Ring them up . . . do you think it will work?

Vet: *(irritated)* It should . . . it's already worked with me!

Captain Oates

by Laurie Rowley

Workmen: Rikki Fulton and others.

Inside a tent, four men wearing parkas with hoods and gloves and boots, sit huddled, trying to keep warm. A freezing gale can be heard outside.

First Workman: *(with stiff upper lip)* Gentlemen, I am going out now and I may be gone for quite some time.

He steps out of the tent. From outside we see it is a workman's tent near some 'Road Works' signs in the High Street. He checks his watch then nips smartish into a pub.

The Old Man and the Priest

by Quentin Reynolds

Priest: Rikki Fulton
Old Man: Gregor Fisher

A party is in progress. We see a very old man approach a priest who is standing trying to hide his glass of whisky with his hat. The old man sidles up to him.

Old Man: Father!

Priest: Yes, my son?

Old Man: I want tae confess . . . I'm eighty-two!

Priest: Age is not in itself a sin my . . . er . . . child.

Old Man: It's not that Father, you see, I've just made love tae a twenty-one-year-old dolly bird wi' kinky boots.

Priest: Kinky boots?

We see his hand shake below his hat and hear the ice cubes rattling round the glass.

Priest: But you are not of the faith, ye lucky - my boy . . . why are you telling me this?

The old man collapses on top of the priest with his arms round him and slowly slides down to the floor.

Old Man: It's no just you Father, I'm tellin' everybody!

Supercop and the Alien

by Bob Black and Laurie Rowley

Supercop: Rikki Fulton
Alien: Gregor Fisher

A typical street corner in the evening. On a wall 'NO PARKING AT ANY TIME'. Parked at the kerb is a futuristic spaceship. Flashing lights, drifting smoke, eerie and unearthly. In charge is an Alien. Dressed in silver with a green face, he has a control panel on his chest. Supercop arrives on his motorcycle and dismounts. He comes over to the spaceship, taking off his goggles in the usual way. He walks around the spaceship. The Alien appears.

Supercop: Ye cannae park here - double yellow lines.

The Alien looks at him but doesn't speak.

Supercop: I say, 'Nightrider!' Ye cannae stop here. You've no licence plate, no tax disc. You are contravening section thirteen, fifteen and 104A of the Road Traffic Act. Savvy?

There is still no answer from the Alien. Supercop looks officious 'Not to be messed about with', and takes out his notebook.

Supercop: I see. Refusing to co-operate. Right, I'll have to take a few particulars, but I must warn ye! Anything ye say will be written doon and used against ye!

Alien: Gflezzglezxtpzzle!

Supercop! Aye, except that! *(he looks at the Alien suspiciously)* You're no fae roond here, are ye? Where ye fae? Somewhere exotic is it? Like Drumchapel? I mean, that's a fancy foreign car, intit? I thought for a moment it wis the Pope Mobile!

Alien: Zzglbgglzztzzt!

Supercop: Have you been on the bevvy pal?

The Alien presses a few buttons on his chest panel. Now he speaks.

Alien: Silence earth being! Cease your pathetic prattling!

Supercop: *(suspiciously)* Are you a poof? Here, whit wis that you pressed?

Alien: This is an intergalactic translator! It allows us to communicate, and lets you comprehend my language.

Supercop: *(fascinated, and much more friendly)* Is that right? An intergalactic trans . . . here, that's marvellous. Would it work wi' the telly? I cannae understand these 'Eastenders'.

Alien: *(grandly)* I am Kwaire!

Supercop: *(steps back quickly)* Aye, I thought that. I'm a happily married man!

Alien: My *name* is Kwaire! I have come from Jupiter, past Saturn and Mars, on my way to Uranus!

Supercop: Here you, don't be cheeky!

Alien: But I was forced to land here. I had some nasty trouble with asteroids!

Supercop: You should have had them out when you were young. *(licks his pencil)* Anyway, gies yir full name and address - and don't forget the post code!

Alien: You fool! I have no post code! I am an Alien and you will not stop me in my mission!

He pulls out a lethal looking ray gun and points it at Supercop.

Supercop: Naw, naw, I don't need a torch. I'll just stand under this light.

He walks over to a lampost, then pauses to write.

Alien: This is not a torch! It is a Brain Cell Disintegrator! It will reduce your brain to the size of a child's! You will become a toddler again! A helpless whimpering baby of five!

The Alien fires the gun and Supercop is engulfed in blue light. He looks at the Alien and gives a dismissive unimpressed sniff.

Supercop: You cannot be serious! Did you think it was gonnae work? Did ye? Did ye really think *that* wee torch was gonnae turn me, a man of my intelligence and superior intellect - a man who watches '3-2-1' and 'The Krypton Factor' every week withoot fail, did you really think it would turn me intae a baby? A toddler? A child of five?

He walks past the Alien towards his bike. Very smug. Very threatening.

Supercop: Well in that case, pal, you are in big trouble. Big BIG trouble!

Alien: Why?

Supercop: *(in a child's voice)* 'Cos I'm gonnae get my Daddy tae you!

Party Time

by John Byrne

Donnie: Rikki Fulton
Donna: Judith Sweeney

The party is in full swing. Donnie approaches Donna.

Donnie: Hi, gorgeous . . . d'ye fancy a boogie?

Donna: *(chewing gum)* Whit's up . . . did ye furget yur hanky?

Donnie: Naw, naw . . . d'ye want tae get on down an' gie it the auld . . . *(he crouches and shoogles).*

Donna: Lay an egg, ye mean? Naw, thanks.

Donnie: Dancin' . . . Ah'm talkin' aboot dancin' . . . d'ye fancy?

Donna: Drap deid, ya four-eyed dumplin'.

Donnie: Cannae quite make up yur mind, eh? Listen, ma pasadoble wis greatly admired last year in Torremolinos . . .

Donna: Ye shouldnae huv hud it hingin' oot then, should ye?

Donnie: Eh?

Donna: Look, gonnae no' staun there, yur takin' the good away fae ma outfit. Away ower there an' ask that wee wumman tae dance . . . hur wi' a face like an upside doon cake . . .

Donnie: Ah'm no dancin' wi' hur . . . that's the manager's wife.

Donna: So where's the manager?

Donnie: Yur lookin' at him.

Donna whisks Donnie on to the dance floor.

Emergency Operation

by Bob Black

Ambulance Man: Rikki Fulton
Doctor: Tony Roper
Nurse: Annette Staines

In the doctor's office an ambulance man is speaking to a doctor and a nurse. They all look very disappointed.

Ambulance Man: *(shaking his head, demoralised, grave)* I . . . I'm sorry, doctor. We did our best. The siren and the flashing lights cleared the traffic ahead of us . . . We went through a red light at eighty miles an hour, but a car coming in the opposite direction forced us to swerve on to the pavement . . . We had to make a detour through the pedestrian precinct, and by the time we got back to the hospital . . .

He lays a newspaper parcel on the doctor's desk.

. . . your chips were cold!

A Bad Match

by Andy Hamilton

Manager: Rikki Fulton
Sammy: Gregor Fisher
Youth: Gerard Kelly
Englishman: Finlay Welsh

In the office of the manager of Glasgow Rangers F.C. The manager is working quietly at his desk filling in his football coupon. Enter Sammy, a talent scout.

Sammy: I've got him outside, boss. That youngster I was telling you about. He's so quick he makes Dalglish look like Ben Nevis. He's brilliant. All the big clubs are after him. I watched him last Saturday. He scored seven times in the first half!

Manager: Well get him in and let's sign him up quick.

Sammy ushers in a nervous looking youth.

Manager: *(holding out his hand)* Pleased to meet you. Sammy's told me all about you, so I think we can dispense with any formalities. I've got a five year contract prepared if you'd just care to sign . . .

Youth: Fantastic! *(he begins to sign the contract).*

Manager: Sammy here says you got seven in the first half on Saturday?

Youth: *(still signing)* That's right. Too bad I missed the second half.

Manager: Why was that! Did you get injured?

Youth: *(having just finished signing the contract)* No, I had to go to Mass.

Manager: *(after a long stunned pause) . . . Mass?*

Youth: Well, I couldn't skip it really, not with my brother being Cardinal and all.

Manager: *(still stunned)* . . . Sammy, how long have you been a scout with Rangers?

Sammy: *(enthusiastically)* Just two days, boss, but what a first signing, eh?

Youth: I must say I was a bit surprised, I didn't think Rangers signed catholics.

Manager: *(falsely benign)* . . . is that so?

Youth: Still, it's all down in black and white now, eh. A legal contract, binding on both sides etcetera.

Manager: True . . . true . . . of course the contract would be rendered null and void if we were to discover, say, that you had a poor disciplinary record.

Youth: You've no worries there. Never been sent off in my life.

Manager: Oh . . . booked?

Youth: No, never.

Manager: Ever nearly been booked?

Youth: No.

Manager: Ever fouled anyone?

Youth: Can't say I have.

Manager: Ever thought of fouling anyone?

Sammy: I tell you, boss, he's an exemplary character on and off the field.

Manager: Sammy . . .

Sammy: Yes, boss?

Manager: Shut up. *(turning to the youth)* Of course you do realise that even though we've put you on a five-year contract, it may be some time before you play for the first team.

Youth: How long?

Manager: Six years.

Youth: I don't mind, it's worth it for the pride of being able to tell the whole world that I, the fourteenth son of a poor catholic family, have been signed up by the great Glasgow Rangers.

Manager: Only provided you can prove your fitness. For instance, if you had some injury . . .

Youth: Never missed a game.

Manager: Hm . . . measles?

Youth: Sorry?

Manager: A bit of a rash, perhaps? Flu? A cold? . . . Plooks?

Youth: Ah well . . .

Manager: *(triumphantly)* Aye. He's had plooks!

Youth: No, not really.

Sammy: Take it from me, boss, this lad is super fit.

Manager: Sammy . . .

Sammy: Yes, boss?

Manager: Shut up. *(turning to the youth)* Well I'm sure you'll pass the necessary club medical with flying colours, lad. It only remains for me to welcome you to the Club. Would you like a cigar to celebrate? *(he opens a box of cigars).*

Youth: Thanks very much.

The manager suddenly slams down the lid on the youth's fingers. The youth wails in agony.

Manager: Can you take this lad down for his medical, Sammy? Just to check he has no physical defects of any kind. Especially about his hands.

Sammy leads the wailing youth away and then re-enters.

Sammy: I hope that accident doesn't affect the lad's medical.

Manager: *(sarcastically)* Oh, me too.

Sammy: Here, boss, I've got another lad outside. He's terrific, watched him midweek. He got a hat-trick inside the first ten minutes. He'd fit in perfectly here.

Manager: Is he a one-legged rabbi? . . .

Sammy: *(very puzzled)* No?

Manager: A Tibetan lama?

Sammy: No?

Manager: An African chief? Or a Spanish hermaphrodite? Only I'm warning you, Sammy, if I find him unsuitable for the image of this club, you'll be picking up your cards and no messing.

Sammy: He's O.K., I'm telling you. I'll fetch him in.

Sammy leaves the room.

Manager: *(pondering)* Ah well . . . what could possibly be worse than a catholic?

Sammy re-enters with an English, tweedy, cricket-type aristocrat.

Englishman: *(obnoxiously public school)* Tally-ho. Spiffing to meet you, bozzers old thing, anyone for soccer?

Manager: *(staring in amazement)* . . . Sammy.

Sammy: Yes, boss?

Manager: Pick up your cards on the way out.

Supercop Meets an Old Friend

by Colin Bostock-Smith

Supercop: Rikki Fulton
Driver: Gregor Fisher

Supercop has just pulled a driver into the side of the road. He gets off his bike and strolls over.

Supercop: Okay, Stirling, I made it sixty-five. What did you make it?

Driver: Sorry officer. I suppose you're right.

Supercop: I'm always right, sunshine. Oot o' the car.

As the driver gets out the car, Supercop gets a good look at him for the first time and does a long double take.

Supercop: Good Heavens! Jock Macilveney!

Driver: *(equally surprised)* Well I'm blessed! Wee Andy Ross! Ah havenae seen you since we left school!

They shake hands.

Supercop: Fantastic to see you, Jock.

Driver: Fantastic to see you, Andy! Well, well, so you're in the polis?

Supercop: Aye - that's why I'm in the uniform! *(they laugh).*

Driver: *(confidentially)* Well . . . listen Andy. For the sake of all the good times we used to have . . . will you let me off the ticket?

Supercop: *(solemnly)* Oh, I wish I could, Jock. But I am an honourable policeman. I cannae do it.

Driver: Andy, please! This'll be my third endorsement. I'll be disqualified.

Supercop: I cannae do it. I cannae.

Driver: But I'll lose my job, man!

Supercop: No, Jock. I cannae do it.

He gets out his pencil and notebook.

Supercop: Now let's see . . . name, Jock Macilveney . . .

Driver: Well . . . you were never really one of the lads, anyway. You were always a big fearty.

Supercop: Who was a big fearty?

Driver: You were! I remember you - never had the guts to do anything!

Supercop: *(outraged)* What? Now listen here, Macilveney, who do you think it was who threw the stone through the baker's window, eh? Me, pal! Me!

Driver: That was nothing.

Supercop: Then what about the shoplifting in Woollies, eh? Who pinched twenty-eight bars of chocolate in one afternoon, eh?

Driver: You never did!

Supercop: I did so! And who put sugar in the minister's petrol tank? Who lit the fire that burned down the sports centre? And who got wee Maggie McCann into trouble and never paid a penny? And who stole the poor box in the . . . in the . . . in . . .

Gradually he realises how he has incriminated himself and stutters to a halt, aghast. Slowly he tears the sheet out of his notebook.

Supercop: Fantastic to see you again, Jock.

The driver gets back into his car.

Driver: Fantastic to see you again, Andy.

The car drives off.

A Dog's Life

by Philip Differ

Old Man: Gregor Fisher
Housewife: Claire Nielson

In a kitchen, a well-to-do housewife with diamond rings, make-up, blue rinse etc. is emptying a tin of 'Laddie' dog food into a bowl. A caption reads 'Mrs. Sidebottom from Bradford'.

Housewife: My Sandy swears by Laddie, he really laps it up. It's got added vitamins to ensure all-round bounce and energetic vitality. And what's more, a large tin of Laddie lasts for days and days and at only 25p a tin, that means I can save enough on house-keeping to . . . *(indicates her jewels)* . . . treat myself now and again. . . Here's your din-dins, Sandy.

She puts the bowl down on the table in front of a very ill looking frail old man who is wearing a tatty dressing gown. He gives a weak acknowledgement.

Sexy Santa

by Bob Black

Santa: Rikki Fulton
Woman: Claire Nielson

An attractive woman is lying in a double bed. Bare shouldered, blankets clutched around her. She is sultry, sexy and seductive. She is speaking to a man who isn't in bed.

Woman: Mmmmm . . . that was wonderful. I wanted it to be so special for you. Did you enjoy it?

Santa Claus beside the bed, pulling his trousers on.

Santa: Aye, lovely. I usually only get a glass of milk and a biscuit!

The Monster

by Peter Moir Fotheringham

The Monster: Rikki Fulton
Baron Frankenstein: Gregor Fisher

In the laboratory of Baron Frankenstein, strapped to a reclining operating table, almost upright, is the 'Creature' . . . Big boots, suit five sizes too wee, the scrubbin' brush hairdo, the bolt through the neck . . .
The Baron makes a final check . . . the strap round the monster's chest, the connection to the generator . . . then he throws the switch.
We hear an organ play and a storm raging outside.
A spark leaps across the terminals . . . there is thunder and lightning . . . a terrible cry. The monster jerks spasmodically into life. The Baron releases the switch.

Monster: Master . . .

Baron: He speaks! My creature speaks!

Monster: Master . . .

Baron: *(eagerly)* Yes? Yes?

Monster: *(looking down at the leather straps across his chest)* Whit's this? Ah thought Ah jist came in furra fillin'?

Baron: No, no . . . you are not at ze dentist's my friend . . . you are in ze laboratory . . .

He starts to unbuckle the straps.

Monster: Aw, that's a loat better . . . *(he rubs his chest)* Where'd ye say Ah wis, pal?

Baron: Ze laboratory . . . I haff pulled you back from ze edge of ze abyss . . .

Monster: Ah hud ma heid doon the pan again, aye? Sufferin' God . . . Tell me, is the party still gaun oan doonsterrs?

Baron: What party? Zerr is no party, my friend . . . you are hallucinatink. I haff only just created you . . .

Monster: Yuv whit???

Baron: I, Baron Frankenstein, haff created you . . . not in my own image, perhaps, but . . . you are my creation. I haff taken ze torso of a weightlifter . . . ze legs of an athlete . . . ze brain from a genius . . .

The monster walks over and looks at himself in a mirror.

Monster: Where d'ye get the herrcut . . . affa badger? That is hellish. An luk whit's stickin' froo ma froat!

Baron: Ah . . . I must apologise for zat . . . I ran out of ze catgut for stitching, so I haff to use ze nut and ze bolt . . .

Monster: Naw, naw . . . Ah like it . . . Ah like it. *(he admires himself in the mirror)* Ah jist hope Senga disnae brek hur wallies oan it when wur neckin' . . .

Baron: Senga?

Monster: Wee Senga McCutcheon fae Pollok . . . ma fiasco.

Baron: No, no . . . you can haff no memory of zis woman . . .

Monster: You must be jokin' pal . . . wance seen never furgoat, Wee Senga. Is she at the party?

Baron: I keep telling you . . . zerr is no party!

Monster: Naw? So how come thur's a strong whiffa alcohol in the air? An' ma heid's nippin' like somebody's jist sawed the tap aff it?

Baron: . . . ze alcohol vos merely for sterilising ze instruments . . .

Monster: Aw, thur's a band, is there?

Baron: And your head hurts only because I am transplanting your brain .

Monster: Eh?

Baron: You did not haff a brain, my friend . . . I am just after giving you von . . . ze brain of von of ze great geniuses of zis vunderful country of ours!

Monster: *(delighted)* Ye mean . . . ?

Baron: Correct. Herman Van Strudelbhom. . .

Monster: Herman Van whit? Since when wis Herman Van whitsisname wanna Scotland's greatest geniuses? Ah thought ye wur talkin' aboot Andy Cameron or Kenny Dalglish . . .

Baron: Vot are you talking about? I said *zis* great country of ours . . . Transalbania . . .

Monster: Transalbania? Ye mean wur no in Castlemulk?

The monster rushes to the window.

Baron: It iss no good looking out ze window, my friend . . . all you vill see is ze barren vastes . . . ze ruined shacks . . . und ze odd peasant lying in ze street . . .

Monster: *(looking out of the window again)* We ur in Castlemulk!

Baron: Come over here und haff a look at vot I am preparing for you . . .

Monster: Is it something nice?

Baron: *(whipping a sheet off a table)* You see!

He reveals a grotesque female monster with strange pointed breasts.

Monster: Aaaaaaaaaaaargh!

The Monster begins to laugh.

Baron: You find her comical?

Monster: No, conical, conical . . . gettit?

Monster: *(to the female monster)* Hullorerr, gorgeous . . . dis yur maw come fae Ireland ur wur yur teeth always that colour?

Baron: I am afraid she cannot answer yet . . . I haff not yet found her brain . . .

Monster: If ye come across two, haud oantae wan fur Senga, wull ye?

Baron: Everysink must be perfect!

Monster: Talkin' aboot things bein' perfect, Prof. . . . ye huvnae any throat sweeties oan ye . . . Ah think Ah must huv a frog or somethin' . . . *(fingering his bolt)* Here, wait a minute, ye didnae go an' . . . .

Baron: No, no, my friend . . . zat is just your new vocal chords settling down . . .

Monster: New vocal chords?

Baron: I haff provided you with ze most *Divine* singing voice in ze Vestern Vorld!

Monster: Aw. terrific! Ah always wanted a singin' voice . . .whose vocal chords wur they . . . Gigli's?

Baron: No . . .

Monster: Pavarotti's? . . . Plastico Domingo's?

Baron: No, no, no, no . . . .

Monster: Whose then?

Baron: Try zem out . . .

The monster opens his mouth and bursts forth with 'When you and I were young Young Maggie' in the voice of Sydney Devine.

The Delinquent Tortoise

by Robert Sykes Andrews

Man: Rikki Fulton
Vet: David Hayman

A vet is seated at the desk in his office. A man enters and sits down, clutching a tortoise.

Vet: Good evening - what seems to be the trouble?

Man: *(lays the tortoise on the desk)* It's Torty, doctor.

Vet: Uh-huh. Let's have a look. What seems to be the trouble with him?

Man: Well, lately, he's been behaving rather strangely.

Vet: Behaving strangely?

Man: Yes. You see, it all began a few months ago. Up till then Torty was just like any other normal tortoise. He spent his days in the garden, chewing lettuce leaves, hiding in the rhubarb . . . I mean, he was an exemplary pet, really, a healthy, well balanced, four-legged reptile - the pride and joy of myself and Doris - that's my wife. She's a semi-invalid, her legs go from under her every now and again, and the rest of her body is a breeding-ground of incapacitating diseases. Well, Torty endeared himself in our hearts so much that he was more than compensation for the family we were never able to conceive on account of Doris never feeling up to it. But suddenly, just after his sixteenth birthday, Torty's whole attitude to life changed.

Vet: Changed? In what way?

Man: Well, instead of pottering about the garden looking for succulent vegetation, he took to lying around the house all day, watching telly, and listening to punk rock records. It got so he wouldn't go near the garden, except at nights, and as we later discovered, only to read a collection of pornographic magazines under the street lamp.

Sometimes he wouldn't come home till the small hours, and invariably with the smell of drink on his breath. We tried giving him lettuce leaves again, only instead of eating them, he rolled them up in a cigarette paper and smoked them.

Then he sat staring at the patterns on the wallpaper with a glazed look in his eyes. Doris and I tried to reprimand him, but he just lay there, sprawled out on the settee, blowing smoke rings, saying 'Don't bug me man.' Then to crown it all, he got our neighbour's tortoise into trouble and refused to stand by her. And this winter, instead of hibernating, he went to Aviemore - to go ski-ing, he said, but we learned from some of his friends who spent Xmas there that he had been running wild through the heather with a gang of criminally insane weasels.

The consequence of all this, doctor, is that I'm at my wits end. And Doris has had to take to her bed with a creeping rash on her thighs and her hair falling out. You're our only hope, doctor. Just what is the matter with him?

The vet rises to examine the tortoise with a stethoscope.

Vet: Well . . .

Man: Approach him with caution, doctor. It wouldn't surprise me if he's got a flick knife hidden up his shell.

The vet examines the tortoise carefully.

Vet: Mm. Well, I'm afraid your tortoise is showing all the symtoms of advanced delinquency.

Man: But I don't understand - Doris and I have given Torty as fine and loving a home as any tortoise could wish for. He's never wanted for anything. How could he turn out like that?

Vet: I think he's just plain rotten, through and through. He may even have psychopathic tendencies.

Man: *(in despair)* Can't you do anything for him?

Vet: I'm afraid not. Had you brought him sooner, a good duffing-up might've helped. But he's too far gone now.

The vet takes a revolver from the drawer in his desk.

Man: You don't mean . . . ?

Vet: It's the only way. It's only a matter of time before he's painting swastikas on his shell and forming a motor cycle gang - just think - Hell's Tortoises. Nobody would be safe from his rampagings. You wouldn't want that on your conscience, would you?

The vet offers the man the gun.

Man: Oh no, I couldn't, I just couldn't.

Vet: I understand.

The vet picks up the gun and the tortoise and leaves the room.

Man: *(sobbing)* Oh Torty . . . oh Torty.

The vet re-enters, holding the gun. His eyes are glazed, and he slowly keels over the desk, a flick-knife embedded in his back. He manages a dying croak.

We hear the noise of a powerful motorbike taking off outside.

A look of horror passes across the man's face.

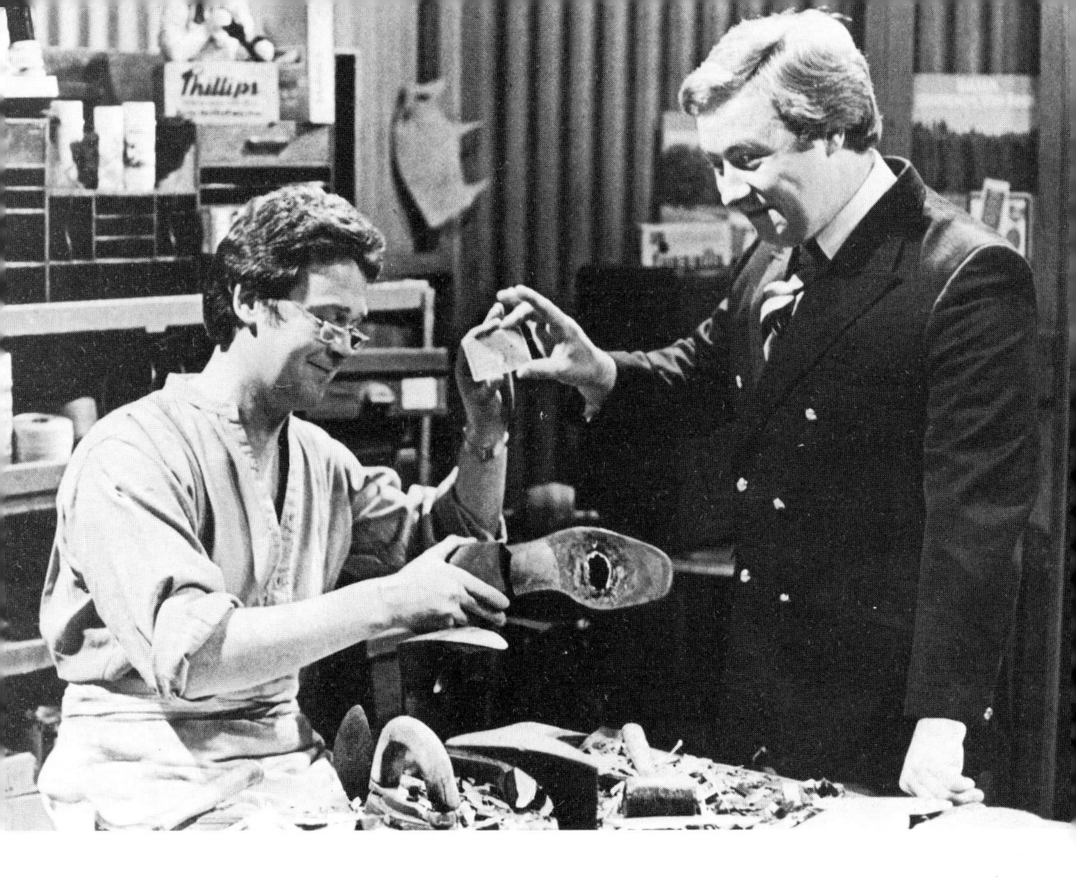

American Express

by Ray Price

Cobbler: Tony Roper
Man: Gregor Fisher

A cobbler is doubtfully examining a man's shoe which has a large hole in the sole.

Cobbler: It would be very expensive to repair sir. It might be cheaper to buy another pair.

The man smugly holds out a plastic card.

Man: American Express?

Cobbler: That'll do nicely, sir.

He takes the card and hammers it over the hole.

In Search of Nessie

by Andy Hamilton

Guide: Rikki Fulton
Hank: Finlay Welsh
Cindy: Claire Nielson

A Highland tourist guide leads an American couple on to a rocky headland.

Guide: Just come this way . . . And of course, the other very famous feature of Loch Ness is its depth. At its deepest point it is . . .

Hank: Excuse me. I want to make a complaint.

Guide: *(wearily)* A complaint?

Hank: Yeah, well y'see . . . Take a look at your brochure. See what it says? 'Round trip to Loch Ness. Sighting of monster guaranteed.'

Cindy: Guaranteed!

Guide: Yes, yes, you'll certainly see her, O.K.?

Cindy: But when?

Guide: I promise you, you'll see *(suddenly he points behind them)* There she is! Oh you missed her. Never mind, perhaps the next trip, eh? We run one every day and . . .

Hank: Hey, hey, hold it, hold it. There's who?

Guide: The monster. She was there.

Cindy: I didn't see her.

Guide: Well I did!

Hank: Yes, but we didn't.

Guide: Well it's not my fault if you're not quick enough is it?

Hank: The brochure distinctly says 'Sighting of the monster guaranteed.'

Cindy: Guaranteed!

Guide: O.K., but it doesn't stipulate who has to do the sighting, does it? *(suddenly pointing)* There she goes again. Too late, she's gone, hard luck.

Hank starts to get angry.

Hank: Now look here, fella. I paid twenty-five pounds sterling to see the Loch Ness monster, not to play peekaboo. Now unless we see the monster, we're going to want our money back. Either that or I'll call the police.

Guide: O.K., O.K., you'll see the monster. Just be patient.

The guide turns towards the bus parked at the side of the road and calls out to the driver.

Guide: Angus, we're having a bit of trouble here. It'll need to be plan B.

The Americans confer briefly. The guide returns to them.

Hank: I mean it. No monster, no money.

Cindy: When are we going to see the monster?

Guide: Look lady. Ever since the dawn of time when she crawled out of the primeval slime, Nessie has eluded the gaze of humanity. Over a span of centuries she has only been spotted by a chosen few. For years and years the world's top scientists have been searching with infinite patience - sometimes decades have passed without even a glimpse of her.

Hank: How long will we have to wait?

Guide: About five minutes.

Cindy: That's very specific.

Guide: Local knowledge. All to do with the tides.

The Guide has started to look impatiently out into the loch.

Cindy: How big is the monster?

Guide: *(still peering out)* Not very.

Cindy: How big is 'Not very'?

Guide: Well . . . you know Angus our coach driver?

Cindy: Yes?

Guide: About the same size as him.

Hank: . . . That's not very big for a monster.

Guide: Look, Mr. Attenborough. Monsters come in all shapes and sizes, O.K.? Some are large, I grant you. Some are not so large. Nessie happens to be coach-driver size. Alright . . . and there she is now.

Hank: Who?

Guide: Ang . . . Nessie! See that blobbish form moving across the water about five hundred yards out?

Cindy: It's not easy to make much out.

Hank: It looks kinda human to me. I'll check it out with my high-powered binoculars.

Guide: *(appalled)* 'High-powered' . . . binoculars!

Hank: These can magnify anything up to five hundred times.

Guide: I wouldn't use those . . . er . . . um . . . you'll just magnify the glare off the water!

Hank: *(smugly)* They're polarised. . . . Say, yeah, I see it. A sort of pink hump in the water, like a stomach.

Guide: Perhaps we'd better leave it. We don't want to disturb her.

Hank: *(still looking)* And in front of the hump . . . a snorkel. *(he looks suspiciously at the Guide).*

Guide: That's not a snorkel, that's an antennae.

Hank: Do you expect me to believe that? That's not a real monster!

Cindy: Yes it is Hank, look, there's another larger one.

A prehistoric-sounding roar echoes across the loch.

Guide: Oh . . . my . . . God!

Hank: Wowie! But he's a biggie! He must be at least forty feet long.

Cindy: Where's the camera?

The Guide stands frozen in dumb horror.

Hank: Say, the big fella's going for the little one. *(more roars)* Listen to that!

Guide: *(covering his face with his hands)* Oh God . . . sorry Angus.

There are distant cries of 'Help - Hughie - Help.'

Cindy: The little one's bellowing back now. He must be a younger monster, his voice hasn't broken yet.

Guide: But I think everything else has.

Hank: This is more exciting than 'Jaws'. Reckon the big fella's won, Can't see the little pink one anymore.

Cindy: Oh how thrilling! Just wait till I get these photos printed.

The Guide is standing motionless. As white as a ghost.

Hank: Thanks fella. That was fantastic. Here's an extra £25.00. Absolutely terrific.

The Guide lifts his head and acknowledges receipt of the money.

Cindy: Oh I can't wait to ring the folks back home, it's so exciting. How soon before we get back to the hotel?

Guide: Just as soon as they can send out a new coach driver.

The Americans have already left. Absolutely thrilled.

The House Call

by Bob Black

Man: Rikki Fulton
Woman: Claire Nielson
Doctor: Gregor Fisher

A sick man lies in bed, feverish and delirious. His anxious wife bends over him, wiping his brow. The man talks and mumbles in his feverish state.

Man: *(only semi-conscious . . . rambling)* Wee glaikit timrous . . . no, no . . . sleekit . . . wee *sleekit* cowerin' . . . is that right . . . cowerin'? Aye . . . wee sleekit glaikit cowerin' amorous beastie . . . oh, what a . . . what a bonnie wee thing, canny wee thing . . . *(sits up)* Canny wee! Oh, wad some flower the giftie gie us . . . flower?

Woman: There, dear . . . *(she mops his brow).*

Man: My love is like a red, red somethin' or other . . . nose . . . aye, nose . . . my love is like a red red nose comin' through the rye . . . an' a man's a man for Auld Lang Syne . . .

Just then the doctor arrives. The woman leads him to her husband's bedside, much relieved. The man continues muttering his verses.

Woman: Oh, doctor, thank heavens . . . he's been like this for hours.

Man: The best played schemes o' rice an' hens gang aft a gangley . . .

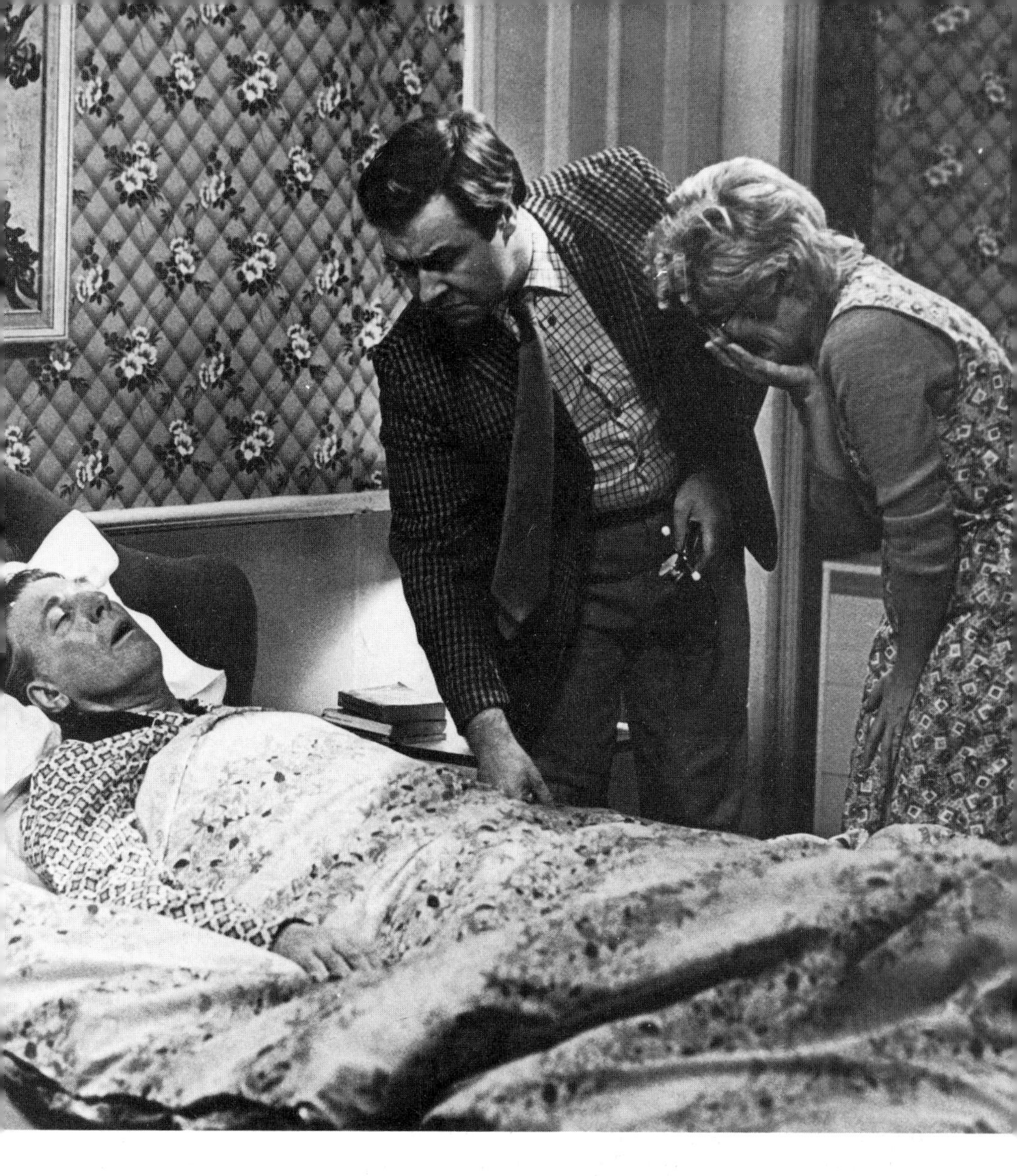

Doctor: *(sounding the man . . . gravely concerned)* You were right to call me Mrs. McAllister . . .

Woman: It's not . . . ?

Doctor: I'm afraid so . . .

Man: Gin a fuddy meet a duddy . . .

Doctor: Your husband's suffering from terrible Burns.

The Gigolo

by Colin Bostock-Smith

First Gigolo: Rikki Fulton
Second Gigolo: Tony Roper
Lady: Claire Nielson

The scene is an old-fashioned dance floor, a sort of 'Palm Court', and a tango is being played by a string quartet.
The lady sits at a table. She is dressed in an old-fashioned style, but is definitely mutton-as-lamb. She is middle-aged-to-elderly, but looks around brightly.
The Gigolo enters. His evening dress is a travesty. One sleeve is much longer than the other. His hair is slicked back in greasy waves. He is slightly drunk and belligerent. He is Scottish. A canvas kit bag hangs from his shoulder.

Gigolo: *(whistles)* Hey, you!

Lady: Ah, are you addressing me, young man?

Gigolo: Yeah, you. C'mon! *(he beckons to her).*

Lady: I beg your pardon?

Gigolo: *(insistent)* C'mon! on yir feet.

Lady: *(rising)* Oh, a dance! How delightful!

They begin to dance, very stiffly.

Lady: It's sweet of you to ask me, young man. But I'm no innocent. I know what you are. You are a gigolo. Am I right?

Gigolo: Aye.

Lady: And tell me, dear boy, why have you become a gigolo?

Gigolo: I couldnae get a job on the Corporation.

Lady: How sweet. Now tell me your name. Is it Antoine? Or Maurice? Or perhaps it is Bertrand?

Gigolo: It's Hughie.

Lady: Hughie - how charming. Well, you're certainly an attractive young man, although your dinner jacket seems to be of rather an unusual design.

Gigolo: Aye, ma mither made it for me.

Lady: It's got one arm much longer than the other.

Gigolo: Aye, so's ma mither.

Lady: Never mind. I just love your hair. That glistening scented sheen!

Gigolo: Aye. I'll get hell when ma mither sees the chip pan.

Lady: And I love your trendy male shoulder-bag. What do you carry in it?

Gigolo: Ma piece.

Lady: You don't mean . . .

Gigolo: Naw, naw. You wouldnae carry that in a bag!

Lady: Tonight you must let me buy you supper. Just something simple - les escargot, filet de sole bonne femme, crepes suzette . . .

Gigolo: *(suspicious)* Is that some of that foreign muck?

Lady: But first, let us enjoy our dance. Oh, it is wonderful to dance with you, Hughie - I feel so secure, so safe. What do you feel?

Gigolo: I can feel hot shivers running down ma back.

Lady: Is it love?

Gigolo: Naw - I think ma tea flask's leaking.

Lady: I shall buy you a new one. And I shall buy you other presents. A watch! An eighteen-carat, jewelled, prismatic, digital computerised, solar-powered chronometer.

Gigolo: Could I no have one wi' Mickey Mouse on the front?

Lady: You may have whatever you wish, Hughie. If you will do something for me . . .

Gigolo: What?

Lady: Come back with me to my yacht tonight.

Gigolo: Why?

Lady: Well . . . I have something there for you. Something that will amuse you, excite you, give you intense pleasure.

Gigolo: My God, do you mean you've got a dart board?

The gigolo is smoothly pushed aside by a second gigolo. This one is immaculate in a swish dinner suit. He has mature good looks with slick hair.

Second Gigolo: Excusez-moi . . . if I may cut in . . . ah, Madame! Commes vous-etes charmant! It will give me the greatest pleasure if you will dance with me.

Lady: *(overcome)* Oh . . . of course . . .

First Gigolo: Now wait a minute!

Second Gigolo: *(dismissive)* Imbecile! Allez-vous en! Pffft!

The second gigolo and the lady dance away, leaving the first gigolo standing feeling stupid.

First Gigolo: Will you look at that! Ma bird's been stole - and by ma ain faither too!

Party Pooper

by John Byrne

First Partygoer: Rikki Fulton
Second Partygoer: Tony Roper
Third Partygoer: Gregor Fisher
Girl: Judith Sweeney

Three guys stand drinking at a Christmas party. An ugly girl approaches holding a small Xmas cracker.

Girl: Does anybody want tae pull a wee cracker?

First Partygoer: Aye, bring her in and we'll have a look at her.

Last Call

by Rikki Fulton

Mrs. Ida Closeshave: Rikki Fulton

Mrs. Ida Closeshave: Good evening. I have recently returned from the Horn - if you'll pardon the expression - of Africa, where Gervais - that's my husband by marriage - and I have been missionaries for the past twelve years.

When we were first married, Gervais had a little church right up in the far North West of Scotland, but it was extremely cold there and his stipend was very small. So we opted to become missionaries and I must say the warm climate seems to suit him.

All our time in Africa has been spent living and working among the Ouagadougou tribe. They are pygmies, you know, no more than four feet or so high, and often I would see them wandering naked through the long-stemmed thistle-down with great broad grins on their faces . . . giggling with each other as if something had tickled their fancy.

The name of their village - Ouagadougou - roughly translated, means 'turn left at the cesspool and mind where you put your feet.' Would, alas, that we had known this that first day Gervais and I arrived at the village. As we approached the large wooden entrance gate, all the natives were gesticulating. It was probably the hot weather. Then they started waving at us and shouting 'Woollamooga! Woollamooga!' Taking this to be some sort of greeting, Gervais and I hurried through the gate - and found ourselves up to our knees in Woollamooga!

It was some time before the Ouagadougous ventured near us . . . although they very kindly offered us a little hut to sleep in - just down wind of them.

When we eventually made contact, the witch doctor - a charming man - taught us how to use the Damsoras when entering or leaving the village through the wooden gate. The Damsoras turned out to be a rather large pair of old wellies, and, incidentally, it was Gervais - ever ready with a statistic - who pointed out that the wellies were twenty-seven inches high, and the witch doctor's inside-leg measurement was twenty-two. He didn't go out much. It was probably he, too, who gave them the name of Damsoras.

Many happy days we spent there in Ouagadougou. I taught the children to read and write some sort of basic English and Gervais ran the bingo hall and the casino. I introduced the children to two books, the Bible and, for very good reasons, *Plumb it Yourself* by H.D. Ballcock. In this way they would learn to care for their brethren and at the same time, look after their cistern.

The children were marvellous. What a sense of humour they had. And such great practical jokers. I never knew from one night to the next *what* I would find in my bed. A snake - a scorpion - a tarantula. One night I actually found Gervais. I think the rascals must have put something in his tea. I think he was as surprised as I was.

School, of course, was always out of doors. I would wear a wide cool skirt and blouse and the boys - nothing at all. And let me tell you I have never seen . . . we all learned a great deal from each other. And when we got thirsty I would say to the boys 'Now - up tree, you - get cocoanut.' And, laughing, they'd reply, 'No up tree us -UP YOU!' And so of course I'd have to climb the tree and the boys would stand underneath laughing as they looked up me - up at me.

Ah, those dear boys. Some of them must be eighteen or nineteen now and I can't wait to see how they've grown.

Gervais on the other hand is not so keen to go back. He and the witch doctor, alas, had a slight altercation on one occasion and Gervais lost his temper . . . I'm afraid he told the witch doctor where to stick his wellies. Didn't you, dear?

We see a midget Gervais perched on a coffee table.

The Wedding Speech

by Peter Moir Fotheringham

Father of the Bride: Rikki Fulton
Mother of the Bride: Claire Nielson
The Bride: Annette Staines
The Groom: Gregor Fisher

A top table wedding party. The usual figures - the young married couple, the best man, the bridesmaid, the father and mother of the bride, the mother (only) of the groom and the minister. They're all looking perfectly happy and content.
The father of the bride has a whisky, a glass of wine and a pint of beer in front of him. He is only slightly drunk at the moment.

M.C.: Ladies and gentlemen, pray silence for the Father of the Bride!

A waiter approaches with a bottle of wine on a tray.
The father of the bride stands up. He is slightly tipsy, holding his empty wine glass.

Father: Ladies and gentlemen, it will be my honour to propose a toast, so please make sure your glasses are full . . .

He turns and waves the waiter forward, holding out his glass.

Just a drop.

The waiter pours a little wine into his glass.

Well, a bigger drop than that.

The waiter pours a little more. The father looks at him accusingly.

Are we running short or something?

The waiter gets the message and fills the glass right up to the top. The father feigns surprise.

Oh, goodness, I'll never manage all this!

He takes the drink anyway and begins his speech.

Now . . . I'm sure you'd all agree that the happy couple have had a wonderful 'do' today. And I'm not just saying that 'cos I paid for it. I can honestly tell you I'm not sad at losing a daughter, not when I'm gaining a wonderful son like Brian.

His wife tugs the hem of his jacket. He bends down and she whispers in his ear. He straightens up again.

Sorry. A wonderful son like Roger.

He looks down at his wife again, still uncertain.

Are you sure?

She nods impatiently. He shrugs. He's about to continue his speech when he looks down at her again.

Who was Brian then? Which one was he?

Wife: Just get on with it!

He shrugs, takes a drink, and continues his speech.

Father: *(getting even more drunk)* It's an emotional time when a father sees his daughter in the arms of another man. I've bounced her on my knees many a time, as, I'm sure, has Roger, and I always told her that Mr. Right would come along eventually. *(he smiles fondly)* To think she nearly wasted herself on that big Nigerian who ended up in Peterheid Prison.

The groom is shocked and the bride mortified as he turns and looks at her accusingly.

Fortunately, she saw the light in time, and I'm sure she did the right thing, putting the baby up for adoption. Now there's nothing to come between her and Roger, in the many years of happiness that lie ahead.

The bride and groom are bickering quietly. The groom is very angry, the bride is on the defensive trying to explain.

Obviously her mother and I couldn't be more proud . . . and I'm just grateful that my dear wife came through her 'wee operation' in time to be here with me. Though, I'm sure her gynaecologist would be fizzin' if he knew she was up and about already.

The mother of the bride is affronted and embarrassed, glaring angrily at her husband. He takes another drink from his glass, growing slightly more unsteady.

On the other hand, it is sad that the groom's father is no longer with us, and couldn't see this happy day. Mrs. McGrouther has our sympathy . . .

The groom's mother looks anxious and nervous.

It's almost a year ago that her husband was taken from her. By the lassie who worked at the service station, I believe. Still, wherever they're living together now, I'm sure his Petrol Pump's in good hands, and that he'd wish his boy all the best on this his big day!

The groom's mother has broken down and started crying. She is being comforted by those around her. The father of the bride has finished his wine and takes a drink of his beer now, pressing on regardless.

If I might touch on the bridesmaid now . . . as the best man has been doing for the last twenty minutes under the tablecloth . . .

The best man and the bridesmaid part abruptly, self-conscious and embarrassed. The father has now turned to the bridesmaid.

Rosemary, you look absolutely radiant. No wonder business is going so well for you down Bridge Street on a Saturday night . . .

The best man draws further away from the bridesmaid now, a look of distaste and suspicion on his face. She looks extremely embarrassed. The father of the bride is more drunk now and tugs at his tie.

Phew . . . is it no a bit warm in here?

His wife whispers hoarsely at him, obviously displeased.

Wife: Will you hurry up and sit down? You're behaving like a cretin!

Father: Oh yes, my wife has just reminded me that I haven't mentioned the minister.

He raises his glass in a casual salute to the minister, who is pleased and smiling.

Well done your Holiness, Reverend, er . . . Highness . . . you did awfy well. And if you say those stoatin' magazines in the vestry weren't yours, then that's good enough for me.

The minister turns away, embarrassed and flustered, not knowing where to look. The father of the bride puts down his glass and takes a telegram from his pocket.

Finally . . . before I sit down . . . there's one message to be read out that arrived to late for the best man to include. Roger . . .

The groom is now smiling. He has stopped bickering with his bride.

It's your all-clear from the clinic! You can go on your honeymoon with an easy mind.

The groom is embarrassed now. The bride is shocked and taken aback. They start bickering and arguing again. Father presses on.

So it just remains for me to propose a toast to the two wonderful people who have made this such an enjoyable, meaningful day for me personally . . .

He lifts his glass in a toast.

The bar staff!

Train to Nottingham

by Alisdair McIntosh

Ticket Man: Rikki Fulton
Passenger: Gregor Fisher

At the ticket window in a railway station. A passenger approaches with a heavy cold and stuffed-up nose.

Passenger: Secud class retud to Dottidham please . . .

Ticket Man: What?

Passenger: Secud class retud to Dottidham please!

Ticket Man: Ah. What you need, sir, is a packet of Tunes. Over there at the kiosk . . .

The man goes off to the kiosk and the ticket man serves the next customer. The man returns. He is sucking a sweet. He looks much happier. He takes a deep breath, then says with a satisfied flourish:

Passenger: Second class return to Nottingham please.

Ticket Man: You're too late pal. The last train left a minute ago!

Dirty Washing

by Rikki Fulton

John: Rikki Fulton
Maggie: Margo Cunningham

In the kitchen of a high-rise flat, Maggie is on the balcony, hanging nappies on the line.
A soldier enters, bursting with enthusiasm and lust and pulling a large parcel behind him.

John: Haw, Maggie! Haw Maggie, Ah'm home! After four long weary years, Maggie. Here Ah am, home.

Maggie emerges from amongst the nappies on the clothes line, her mouth full of pegs.

John: Haw, Maggie. Haw, there ye are, Maggie.

He starts scraping the floor like a bull.

John: Four long weary years, Maggie. Four years . . . Is that new teeth ye've got?

Maggie: *(taking the clothes pegs out her mouth)* Naw, stupit. They're clothes pegs. Oh John, four years you've been away. Four long years. D'ye think Ah've changed?

John: Well, Ah would hope so in four years . . . Oh, Ah see whit ye mean . . . Ah thought ye meant yir under . . . Naw, ye huvnae changed. Ye look exactly as ye did the day Ah left. Damn yir rotten luck. Here, Maggie. See whit Ah've got

Maggie: Oh, John. A medal.

John: Aye, see what it says.

Maggie: 'For Honesty, Integrity and Character.' Oh John. How did ye get that?

John: Ah swiped it. But, aw Maggie, it's been four years. Four long years Ah've not saw ye.

He suddenly sees the clothes line full of nappies, and wonders.

Maggie: *(hastily)* Ah'm takin' in laundry, John.

John: Yir takin' in whit?

Maggie: Laundry.

John: My Gawd! - Ah thought ye said ye were takin' in lodgers.

Maggie: Was it awful for ye, John?

John: Awful? Naw - wis great. Made a fortune floggin' fags an' chocolate. Aw, Maggie, it's great tae be home. And now that Ah've saw ye - Ah'm just away doon tae the pub for two or three days.
Oh, here, Ah nearly forgot.

He drags the large parcel forward.

Maggie: For me? Oh, John - ye shouldnae of. Whit is it?

John: Ma dirty washin'.

Coochee-Woochee

by Niall Clark

Man: Rikki Fulton
Woman: Claire Nielson

In the lounge of a suburban house, a horrible, smotherly woman is cuddling a revolting lap dog. An irritated husband stands nearby, pouring himself a drink.

Woman: Is naughty daddy cross with mummy's little coochee woochee? *(she nuzzles the dog)* What did mummy's little darling do?

Man: Mummy's little darling just performed on the carpet.

Woman: Oh that was naughty. Give mummy a kissy. *(she kisses the dog on the nose)* That's better. And what did naughty daddy do?

Man: I rubbed her nose in it.

Whaur's Yir Wullie Shakespeare Noo?

by Rikki Fulton

Cedric: Rikki Fulton
Jinty: Jan Wilson

In a modern kitchen of a multi-storey flat, with table, chairs, cooker etc. Jinty is working at the cooker. She is dressed in skirt, jumper and apron. The phone rings. She answers.

Jinty: Hello? Oh, hello Mary. Coffee at eleven? Yes, fine. What? no, he's not up yet. I was just away to give him a shout . . . Oh, I don't know . . . ever since he joined that damned DRAMATIC CLUB . . . it's like living with Wullie Shakespeare . . . you don't know whether you're in a multi at Clydebank or the castle at Elsinore . . . No . . . *(we hear the toilet being flushed)* Here, I'd better go, I hear rumblings off stage. I think Sir Laurence is about to make his entrance.

She hangs up as Cedric, still in his nightshirt and wearing a great horned hat appears.

Cedric: Goodmorrow, fair midden. *(sings)* It was a lover and his lass, with a hey and a ho, and a hey nonino. *(he slips on a rug)* I nearly went upon my - elky . . . did ye see that?

Jinty: Sit down and have your breakfast.

Cedric: *(feeling one of the horns)* Here, Ah hope that's nothing serious! *(he laughs, then stops abruptly and strikes a pose)* Ah, Cleopatra, I have news for thee. Ceasar has come forth.

Jinty: Oh, has he?

Cedric: Aye, that means there'll be nae place money. *(he laughs again).*

Jinty: What's that you've got in your hand?

Cedric: Marry, I will tell thee. I was about to take leave of my chamber when - of a sudden - there was a crash . . .

Jinty: And?

Cedric: It seems my chamber hath taken leave of me.

He holds up the remains of a chamber pot. Jinty puts a herring on a plate and brings it to the table.

Cedric: Is this a kipper I see before me - it's dead eye glazed yet mocking - it's clammy corpse reeking with a most thunderous stench. I charge thee, wife - something is rotten in the state of Clydebank.

Jinty: What are you talking about? Kipper! It's a herring, stupid. A HERRING.

Cedric: What's in a name. That which we call a herring by any other name would smell as yeugh!

Jinty: *(taking the fish away)* Alright, alright, I gather you don't want the herring. What do you say to an egg?

Cedric: Hello Egg!

Jinty: Do you want an egg or do you not want an egg?

Cedric: Aye, an egg. But SOFT . . . If it were done when 'twere done then, 'twere well that it was done when 'twas done well if 'twere well . . . Aye, gie us an egg.

Jinty puts an egg into boiling water.

Jinty: D'ye want tea or coffee?

Cedric: Hot tea or hot coffee - that is the question. Whether 'tis nobler in the mind to suffer the tang and flavour of P.G. Tips which according to legend hath much attraction for the monkey - Aye, tea good wife, but not too strong.

Jinty pours the tea. It is very watery.

Cedric: The quality of thy tea is strange. It droppeth as the gentle rain from heaven. *(he sings)* I think that I shall never see, a weaker pot of morning tea. Too weak to crawl out of the spout, 'tho there is not the slightest doubt, the water's there it's plain to see, but only God knows - where's the tea?

Jinty brings an egg to the table on a spoon. It falls onto the table with a heavy clunk.

Cedric: *(picking it up and looking at it)* Alas, poor Yorick, I knew him well. He was never laid, he was quarried. But tarry I must, no! I go. Farewell. To the street of Buchanan and Sauchiehall the corner thereof I do attend to wait upon the chariot they call the Number Two. And early there I must always be for 'tis said and said well, that time and a corporation bus wait for no man.

Jinty: *(putting a lunch box into his hands)* Thy piece go wi' ye.

Cedric: *(sniffing the box)* All that festers is not mould - what's in it anyway?

Jinty: Something that'll suit you down to the ground.

Cedric: What?

Jinty: Ham!

How's Yours?

by Bernard Cranwell

Jimmy: Rikki Fulton
Rory: Gregor Fisher

We hear the noise of a wild party in progress as a man and a woman enter a darkened bedroom. They are drunk and giggling. They sprawl across the bed, intent on pleasures of the flesh. Another couple appear from under the sheets. They too are the worse for drink.

Jimmy: Rory!

Rory: Jimmy!

Jimmy: Fancy seeing you here . . . how's the wife?

Rory: Oh she's great. Smashing. How's mine?

The Indian Restaurant

by John Byrne

Cyril McCluskey: Rikki Fulton
Margaret: Judith Sweeney
Waiter: Tony Roper

An elegant couple are seated in an Indian restaurant. He is very snooty, she is a little coy and adoring. Indian music plays in the background. An Indian waiter approaches.

Waiter: Menu, madam?

Cyril: *(airily)* No, no, no . . . I shouldn't think we'll be requiring a menu.

Margaret: But, Cyril . . .

Cyril: Margaret, dear . . . how many times do I have to say it? You are dining out with a sophisticate . . . a gourmet . . . a man of the world . . .

Margaret: *(sweetly apologetic)* Sorry, Cyril . . .

Cyril: My dear girl, what Cyril McClusky doesn't know about the eating habits and culinary tastes of the residents of Bombay and Krishnaphur could be engraved on a . . .

Waiter: . . . single grain of basmati rice?

Cyril: Exactly.

Margaret: *(adoring, admiring)* Oh Cyril . . . I do love you.

Cyril: You've obviously got good taste.

Waiter: Yes Sir?

Cyril: *(to Margaret)* How are ye at handlin' the auld chopsticks, sweetheart? *(to waiter)* Wull huv two o' yur big soup plates o' broon stuff, but no too hot, tell yur cook . . . the last lot Ah hud nearly blew the backside oot ma troosers . . .

Waiter: Vindaloo?

Cyril: Naw. Ah wis in the kitchen at the time.

The Pair of Socks

by Terry Ravenscroft

Customer: Rikki Fulton
Assistant: Steve Pinder

A male assistant stands at the menswear counter in a department store. A customer carrying a plastic bag approaches.

Assistant: Can I help you sir?

Customer: Yes, my wife bought me a pair of socks for Christmas and . . .

Assistant: . . . and you would like to change them?

Customer: That's right, how did you guess?

Assistant: I've got a wife myself sir, and let's face it, wives have got some very peculiar tastes haven't they?

Customer: They certainly have, yes. So it's alright if I change them?

Assistant: By all means sir, by all means - if you'd just let me have them .

Customer: Of course.

He puts his foot up on a chair and starts to remove his shoe.

Assistant: Excuse me sir. What are you doing?

Customer: You did say you'd change them, didn't you?

Assistant: Well, yes, but I didn't realise they'd been worn.

Customer: You're allowed to try them on surely? And it's a good job I did because I think they're a very inferior quality.

He peels off a day-glow bright sock and hands it to the assistant who grimaces at the smell.

There you are, good as new.

Assistant: There's a hole in it!

Customer: *(removing his other sock)* So you agree they're of inferior quality? *(he hands over the other sock. It is a grey one)* Here's the other one . . . and that reminds me . . .

Assistant: It's a different colour!

Customer: They're a bad match as well.

Assistant: I'm sorry sir, these are not a pair of socks.

Customer: You're telling me? I noticed that as soon as I put them on. Terrible oversight by your department.

Assistant: It's not an oversight by us sir because I'm afraid your wife did not purchase these socks in this store.

Customer: Oh but she did purchase these socks in this store.

Assistant: She can't have done. I'm familiar with all our current lines . . . *(indicates the bright sock)* . . . we don't do a sock like this.

Customer: You do and I can prove it - I've got a receipt . . . *(he produces a receipt and points it out)* . . . Look, one pair of socks - eighty-five pence. December the twenty-fourth . . .

Assistant: *(looking at the receipt)* . . . 1980?

Customer: That's right.

Assistant: I thought you said you were only trying the socks on . . . you've been 'trying them on' for three years!

Customer: Well I don't like to make snap judgments. But when I form an opinion I stick to it. And in my opinion, those socks are rubbish.

Assistant: But you've had these socks for three years! That's a long time. Alan Wells won his Olympic gold medal three years ago!

Customer: He wouldn't have if he'd been wearing those socks I can tell you. Worst pair of socks I've ever had.

Assistant: Well I'm sorry sir, but there's nothing I can do.

Customer: You're refusing to change them?

Assistant: I can't, not after three years.

Customer: Typical isn't it? You con innocent people into purchasing your shoddy goods and when it comes to a genuine complaint you don't want to know.

Assistant: That's not true!

Customer: No? Alright then, what about if I'd only had them for a week?

Assistant: Well that would be different.

Customer: *(unfastening his trousers)* Well about these underpants my niece bought for me . . .

The Sex Survey

by Tom Magee-Englefield

Man: Finlay Welsh
Woman: Claire Nielson

A man knocks at a front door which is opened by a woman.

Man: Good evening. Are you Miss Jennifer Hoskins who completed a postal questionairre about your sex life for the Abacus Survey Company?

Woman: Yes I am. Are you from the same survey team?

Man: No, I'm from the *Guinness Book of Records.*

The Lost Dog

by Bob Black

Man: Rikki Fulton
Sergeant: Tony Roper

In a police station a desk sergeant is dealing with a man who is very agitated and upset. The man is almost in tears. The sergeant is attentive and understanding.

Sergeant: Now sir, just calm yourself . . . calm down . . .

Man: I . . . I'm sorry, sergeant. I'm just so worried. He's only a wee dog and he's been gone for hours now! Hours!

Sergeant: Yes, so you said, sir. What's your dog's name?

Man: I call him Precious! He's just a wee poodle . . . I've had him since he was a wee pup . . . *(growing more and more emotional)* . . . we've been together such a long time! He's my life! My whole life!

Sergeant: *(awkward, embarrassed)* Yes, sir . . .

Man: And now he's been gone all night! Since yesterday evening. I'm fair demented wi' grief! *(takes out a handkerchief and blows his nose).*

Sergeant: Can you give us a description of . . . Precious?

Man: Oh aye. He's twelve now . . . eighteen inches high . . . curly black hair, a tartan collar wi' a bell and a coat!

Sergeant: A coat?

Man: *(becoming sentimental)* Aye. A wee blue coat wi' his name on. It ties underneath. It was his birthday present three years ago. The twenty-ninth of May. Precious is a Gemini. He . . .

Sergeant: Yes, yes. Anything else you can tell me?

Man: His booties. Wee woolly socks. He looks so bonny . . . so bonny . . . and now he's gone. I sat up all night just holding his rubber biscuit. His wee basket and dish in the corner. If . . . if anything's happened to him I don't know what I'll do . . . I'll . . .

The man breaks down sobbing into his hankie.

Sergeant: Now, now, I'm sure nothing has happened sir. Just you leave it with us and get yourself off home. We're rather good at this sort of thing.

Man: *(turning to go)* Aye, I suppose so . . . I'll wait till you phone, then. I'll just . . .

He stops suddenly as if just remembering something.

Sergeant: Was there something else, sir?

Man: *(looking back)* Aye. You might keep an eye open for the wife, too. She was with him.

The Consultation

by Bob Black

Patient: Rikki Fulton
Doctor: Gregor Fisher
Nurse: Judith Sweeney

In the surgery of a family G.P. the doctor is at his desk making notes. His nurse is over in the corner replacing files in a filing cabinet. There is an empty chair in front of the doctor's desk.

Doctor: Who's next nurse?

Nurse: Mrs. McPherson, doctor.

Doctor: Fine. If you'd like to give me her file and ask her to . . .

There is a loud banging on the surgery door.

Patient: *(very rude and very angry)* Heh . . . come on, come on. Open up in there! Ah huvnae goat aw day! Open up! Oh . . . pen!

The nurse looks at the doctor in surprise. She crosses and opens the door. The patient enters. He has one leg in plaster. His arms stick out from his body and are supported by rods. a heavy bandage is wrapped round his head. He limps in in a foul mood.

Patient: Aye, an' aboot time tae! Whit's gaun on in here? You an' hur up tae yir shenanigans . . . is that it? Ah've read aboot you doacters . . . is that whit wis happenin' while ootside, a patient . . . a badly injured man . . . has tae hing aboot fur 'oors!

Docter: I'm terribly sorry. Would you like to take a seat?

Patient: Naw, naw . . . Ah'll jist staun here an' dae some body-poppin'. Course Ah'd like a seat!

He limps to the chair and eases himself painfully into it.

Docter: Now . . . er . . . what seems to be the problem?

Patient: Whit seems tae be the problem? Ur ye blind? Can ye no see whit the problem is? Whit dae ye think Ah came tae see ye wi' . . . dandruff? Ah've got a broken leg . . . two broken airms . . . an' a broken heid! That's the problem!

Docter: Dear, oh dear . . . have you had an accident?

Patient: Naw. It wis ma ain decision tae huv a broken leg . . . two broken airms an' a broken heid! Ah sent away fur them oot a catalogue! Ah wis assaulted, ya mug! Several times oan several occasions!

Nurse: Heavens!

Patient: Ah wis at the fitba', wasn't Ah! The Auld Firm gemme . . . aw Ah done wis turn tae this fella in the green an' white muffler an' say 'Ah don't know who you support pal, but if Ah wis a catholic Ah'd haun back ma holy medals . . . thur playin' like a buncha left-fittit nuns wi' cataracts!' *(he shakes his head in amazement).* He hut us atween the shooder blades wi' a boattle o' dilutin' orange an' flang us doon the sterrs! Seemed tae be annoyed or somethin'. Broke ma leg! Look! Ahyah!

Docter: Tch. tch, tch, tch . . . some people do seem to have remarkably short tempers . . .

Patient: Then Ah wis oan the bus . . . the leg's in stookie . . . nut a soul tae gie us a seat, so Ah says tae this punk wi' the mohican herrcut . . . very quietly ye understand . . . 'Excuse me, sir . . . I realise that you huv probably hud a very busy moarnin' sniffin' glue an' pittin' the heid oan auld age pensioners an' vomittin' intae wean's prams but in my young day a boy like yursel' wid staun up an' gie a fellow human being, what has been physically maligned jist fur bein' polite, a seat oan a bus instead of jist sittin' there like a daud o' sub-human filth wi' technicolour lice fawin' oot his manky herr oantae his scabby jaikit!'

He shakes his head again in baffled amazement.

He flang us aff the bus! While it wis gaun! Broke baith ma airms!

Docter: And what . . . er . . . . exactly are you here for now?

Patient: Whit d'ye think Ah'm here fur? Clarinet lessons? Ah'm here fur somethin' medicinal! Ah'm in agony an' terrified tae cough! Get movin'!

Docter: Yes, yes . . . of course . . . I do apologise . . .

Patient: Ah should think so an aw! Ahyah!

Doctor: Nurse . . . the big green capsules, please . . .

Nurse: But, doctor . . . ?

Doctor: Thank you, nurse.

Patient: Ah jist hope these ur powerful enough . . .

Doctor: Oh, they are . . . they are.

Patient: *(to the nurse)* Well, whit're ye waitin' fur? Pap wan doon ma throat right now!

The nurse looks at the doctor . . .

Doctor: Give him two, nurse . . .

Patient: Make it three . . . c'mon, c'mon . . .

The doctor shakes out the capsules onto his tongue while the nurse helps him to a glass of water.

Patient: Aw, that's better . . . well, don't jist staun there! Give us a haun up! Ah can hardly move! An' don't think Ah'm no gonnae complain aboot you! Don't think Ah'm no gonnae phone the Health Board when Ah get hame! Don't think jist because ye gave us a few painkillers . . .

Docter: I didn't give you any painkillers . . .

Patient: Eh? Whit wis them big green pills if they wurnae . . . ?

Docter: Double strength laxative. That should get thing moving. Good morning.

The patient hobbles off fast towards the door.

A Grave Encounter

by Colin Bostock-Smith

John: Rikki Fulton
Edith: Claire Nielson

In the graveyard there are two graves side-by-side, each with a modern, marble headstone. Two people are present, each tending one of the graves. John is a middle aged, rather mousey man. Edith is also middle aged and a similar sort of person. Clearly they do not know each other.

John: Err . . . good afternoon.

Edith: Good afternoon.

John: My first visit. Since the funeral, you understand.

Edith: Mine too. But in future I shall come very regularly.

John: Of course.

Edith: About . . . once a year, I'd say.

John: I just came on the spur of the moment. I was feeling a little depressed and I thought - I know - I'll go and visit the wife's grave. It'll cheer me up.

Edith: It's your wife, is it?

John: Yes. My Mary. . . . Your husband?

Edith: Yes. This is my Michael.

John: The Lord giveth and the Lord taketh away.

Edith: Yes. And sometimes he taketh his time about it.

John: I brought these roses. Mary loved her rose bushes. She loved them more than she loved me. So I cut these this morning, from her own bushes.

Edith: How nice!

John takes secaturs from a bag and clips the roses into little bits and grinds them into the ground with his shoe.

Edith: I brought these flowers for Michael. *(she produces a big bouquet).*

John: Beautiful.

Edith: Yes . . . *(she scatters them on his grave).* You know, Michael always had the most terrible hay-fever. That's a nice marble slab on top of your Mary's grave.

John: Aye. And underneath that it's reinforced concrete.

Edith: I prefer grass myself. I like to think that, as the fresh young grass sprouts from the earth, it is somehow Michael, being born anew.

John: A wonderful thought.

Edith produces garden shears and clips the grass vigorously on the grave.

John: Have you a nice inscription on his headstone, may I ask.

Edith: Oh Yes. 'Thou shalt see me again in Paradise!'

John: Ah . . .

Edith *(under her breath)* But not if I see thee first. Err. . . what's your inscription?

John: 'She is not dead, she only sleepeth.'

Edith: Now that's nice. When did you bury her?

John: Four weeks ago.

Edith: Four weeks?

John: I reckon she should be dead by now.

Edith: Was it . . . sudden?

John: No. *(as if quoting a newspaper death notice)* After a long illness patiently borne . . .

Edith: *(impressed)* Patiently borne . . .

John: Yes, by me. Was your Michael's death sudden?

Edith: Aye, it was. An industrial accident, in a manner of speaking.

John: An industrial accident?

Edith: Aye. They told him they'd got him a job and he died of shock.

John: My wife, she wanted to be buried at sea. For sentimental reasons.

Edith: She liked sailing?

John: No. Sailors.

Edith: I see . . .

John: *(shyly)* We have a lot in common, you and me.

Edith: *(pleased)* Aye, we have . . . *(they look hopefully at each other).*

John: My Mary said, if I ever looked at another woman after her death, she would turn in her grave.

Edith: My Michael said if I ever looked at another man, he'd turn in his grave.

John: . . . . . . Oh well . . . perhaps the exercise will do them good.

Edith: Aye . . .

They walk off happily together.

The Dosser

by Philip Differ

Dosser: Rikki Fulton
Woman: Annette Staines
Man: Tony Roper

A dosser on a street is doing his routine.
A lady comes out of a telephone box.

Dosser: Excuse me, madam, would you like to make a donation to the Save the Dosser Fund?

The woman just ignores him as another man approaches.

Dosser: Excuse me sir, please don't take offence but would you happen to have ten pence for a cup of tea?

Man: *(sighs)* O.K.

He gives him ten pence and makes to walk off.

Dosser: You're a gent sir, a true gent, now at least I'll have a cup of tea, a few bob more and I could maybe have had something to eat as well.

Man: *(hesitates and turns back)* Here, get yourself a bite to eat. *(hands him some more change).*

Dosser: Thank you sir, now I'll feel strong and nourished as I walk the twenty-four miles to see my sick mother because I can't afford the rail fare.

Man: *(thinks a bit, as he see the pathos in the man's expression).* Wait, here you are.

He hands the dosser a few pounds

Dosser: Oh, sir, you bring tears to my eyes, such kindness.

Man: *(slightly embarrassed)* Well, we're all human. It's a sad day when a man can't help his fellow man when he's in need.

Dosser: God bless you sir, that is true. *(he starts to walk off).*

The man smiles, feeling pleased with himself, but suddenly stops and checks his pockets. He shouts and hurries across to the dosser who is counting his money.

Man: Listen, I'm hell of a sorry, but I've left myself without my bus fare, do you think you could . . . *(holding out his hand).*

The dosser, whose attitude has suddenly changed to quite haughty, sticks the money in his pocket.

Dosser: Away and work!

Dining Out American Style

by John Byrne

Gent: Rikki Fulton
Lady: Claire Nielson
Manager: David Hayman
Waitress: Ann Louise Ross

In a trendy new Yankee eaterie in Glasgow there is loud rock music and modern decor. The manager is dressed in western gear. The waitress is dressed in American cub scout shirt, kerchief and blue jeans. A Glasgow couple enter. They are fairly untrendy.

Manager: *(with phony American accent)* Hi there, welcome to Buffalo Benny's . . . A booth for two? Yeah? Okay, right this way . . . *(hands them each a menu)* Hey Candy! *(a waitress appears)* Take these guys' orders. *(addressing the couple)* Coupla Manhattans?

Gent: Naw, naw . . . Two Glaswegians.

Lady: He means a refreshment, Tommy . . . don't let yur ignorance hing oot . . . Aye, I'll huv a Manhattan . . . a big wan.

Manager: And your friend?

The gent has managed to disengage a piece of wood from the booth.

Lady: He'll huv a screwdriver . . . wulln't ye, Tommy?

Gent: Ah'd be better wi' a hammer . . .

Lady: Stoap affrontin' us, you . . . it's a drink . . .

Gent: Aye, a good idea. Ah could dae wi' wan.

The manager retreats to get the drinks. Candy the waitress is close to the gent, showing off her cleavage.

Candy: Yeah?

Gent: Yeah!

Lady: She means ur ye ready tae order?

Gent: Aw.

Lady: *(scanning the menu)* Ah'll huv a Benny's Buffaloburger wi' french fries . . . Tommy?

Gent: Aw . . . er . . . Ah'll huv the same, wi' chips.

Lady: An' a hauf-pun Waffle-weenie.

Gent: Eh?

Lady: It's like a piece oan stovies wi' syrup oan it. 'S terrific!

Candy: Two?

Gent: Oh aye, er . . . naw . . . er . . . Ah'll stick tae the . . . er . . .

Candy: How'd ye like the burgers?

Gent: *(looking at her cleavage)* Oh they're very nice.

Lady: She means how dae ye like the beefburgers.

Gent: Wuv no hud them yet.

Lady: She means cooked.

Gent: Aye, wull huv them cooked.

Candy: Rare? Medium Rare? Medium to well? Well? . . . well?

Lady: *(looking at Tommy)* Well?

Gent: Well *(to waitress)* Well? Whit ye waitin' fur? Ah've already told ye.

Candy: *(writing)* Charred. *(walks off)*.

Lady: How d'ye no stop giein' us a showin' up, you . . . They must think we're a right coupla . . .

The manager breezes in with drinks and sets them down.

Manager: You're welcome . . . *You're welcome.*

Lady: *(nudging gent)* Gie him a tip.

Gent: Whit?

Lady: *(between clenched teeth)* Gie him a tip.

The gent pulls the piece of timber from under the table and hands it to the manager.

Gent: Get yur jiner tae yase stronger glue, pal. Yur joint's fawin' apart.

Lady: *(burying her head in her hands)* Ah'm affruntit. Ah cannae take you anywhere.

The manager moves off, definitely not pleased. Candy returns with the food.

Candy: Half pound Buffaloburger, french fries. Waffle-weenie. *(sets it down).* Half pound Buffaloburger, french fries, potato chips. *(sets it down and exits).*

Gent: Heh . . . thuv dumped a packet o' crisps oan mines . . .

Lady: Aw, shut yur gub an' eat yur dinner.

Candy returns with the relish tray.

Candy: Thousand Island, watermelon pickle, blue cheese . . . pumpernickel, mayo?

Gent: Y'any broon sauce, sweetheart?

Lady: Gawd!

Candy: Sorry?

Gent: Broon sauce . . . furra chips.

Lady: French fries . . . he means fur the french fries.

Gent: An' Ah never asked furra roll . . . *(he holds up the sesame bun)* If Ah'd wanted it oan a piece . . . *(he dangles the bun).*

Lady: Gonnae shuttit?

Gent: *(shutting bun)* Ah never asked furra roll.

Candy: I'll get you a doggy bag. *(exits).*

Gent: But Ah huvnae got a dug.

The manager reappears.

Manager: *(smarmily)* Everythin' ace with you folks?

Lady: Yeah . . . these burgers is really cool.

Manager: *(icily)* And sir's?

Gent: Mine's stone cauld.

Lady: Behave yursel' . . . *(to manager)* Really cool . . .

Manager: Yeah. Max is really into charcoal.

Gent: My God, his hands must be right manky.

Manager: If there's anything else you guys need . . . cheesecake, ice-dreams, chocolate, vanilla, pistachio . . .

Gent: *(getting up)* Aye, Ah think Ah'll away furra quick pistachio. Where's the . . .

Manager: Cowpokes. It's on the door.

Exit the gent in search of the toilet.

Manager: Ah'm no gonnae wind up wi' that mug as a brer-in-law, um Ah? Where d'ye pick them up, oor Myra?

U.F.O.

by Rikki Fulton

Spaceman: Rikki Fulton
Interviewer: Claire Nielson
Newscaster: John Bett

Newscaster: We interrupt this programme to bring you an exciting newsflash. At Hampden Park this evening, the League Cup semi-final was abandoned when an Unidentified Flying Object landed on the centre circle. Our reporter, Peever McIver, has persuaded the . . . the occupant to come into the studio.

The spaceman, wearing a space suit, opens the vizor of his space helmet.

Spaceman: It's been no a bad day!

Interviewer: Er - no, it hasn't, has it? But now, sir, do tell us. We're all agog here - where have you come from?

Spaceman: Me? Oh, Ah've come fae Mars. That's away oot past Gourock there.

Interviewer: You're from Mars, are you? I shouldn't have thought there was any life on Mars.

Spaceman: Oh, well, not durin' the week, maybe, but it brightens up a bit at the weekend.

Interviewer: I see. And how did you learn to speak our language?

Spaceman: Oh, that was easy. We listened to *Take the High Road.*

Interviewer: You mean you can get *Take the High Road* away up there?

Spaceman: Get it? We couldnae get rid of it.

Interviewer: Well, I'm sure we wish you every success. And tell me, how long did it take you to travel here?

Spaceman: Fifteen years.

Interviewer: Fifteen years? Why so long?

Spaceman: Aw, the lights were against us all the way.

Interviewer: And is yours the only saucer to make the trip?

Spaceman: Oh for Gawd's sake, no! Naw, a whole teaset landed in the Pacific. Probably washed up by now. You know, it was funny. There we were, flyin' through space on our way to earth - and we'd come about twenty million miles when Ah turned tae ma mate, an' says, 'Hey Charlie', Ah says, 'Ah'll bet they're no in.'

Interviewer: But we were, weren't we. Tell me, is it enjoyable living on Mars?

Spaceman: No.

Interviewer: But surely you must have some way of amusing yourselves. How do you pass the time?

Spaceman: Oh well . . . *(he laughs lecherously)* And we've got the pictures. And we go to the pub.

Interviewer: I never imagined there would be pubs on Mars!

Spaceman: Oh aye, have ye never heard o' Mars Bars?

Interviewer: Well now, sir, we're all pretty excited about your visit. I mean, it isn't every day a flying saucer lands in Scotland. There must be some very important reason for your visit.

Spaceman: You're dead right, kid. You don't think I've travelled all these millions of miles for nothing, do you? You don't think I'd make that long and hazardous journey if it wasn't of the tantamountest importance, do you? No. I've brought a message of supreme importance from the people of Mars to the people of Earth. It's here - er - no, maybe it's in this one - it's of the greatest urgency, this . . . er . . . Oh, my God! I'll have to go back. I've left it in my other suit.

Testing

by Quentin Reynolds

Archie: Rikki Fulton
Wife: Claire Nielson

We see a man dressed for gardening. Beside him there is a watering can. He is holding a lemonade bottle in each hand, inspecting them, puzzling over the contents. He sets one bottle down on the table and pours his wife, who is seated with a glass in her hand, a drink from the other bottle.

Man: Try that then.

Wife: Thanks Archie.

She drinks the contents of the glass, watched intently by Archie.

Wife: Oh, that cola was nice . . .

Archie lays aside the bottle of cola and picks up the other bottle from the table and gives it a quick glance.

Archie: *(in a matter of fact tone)* This'll be the weed killer then.

He pours the contents of the bottle into the watering can and exits, leaving his wife, speechless with horror.

The Beechgrove Garden

by Laurie Rowley

George: Rikki Fulton
Jim: Gregor Fisher

In a greenhouse in the Beechgrove Garden someone is thrashing about in dense foliage. Suddenly the greenery parts and the two boys appear.

Jim: Hello again and welcome to a very special New Years Eve edition of the Beechgrove Garden . . .

George: Aye, which this week comes to you from . . .

Jim: Which this week comes to you from our greenhouse at Aberdeen Television Centre.

George: We *were* going to Dingwall this week weren't we Jim?

Jim: Aye, but who the hell wants to be in Dingwall on New Year's Eve?

George: Aye, who the hell wants . . . *(forgets the rest).*

Jim: Right George, we're in the middle of winter - not ideal weather for gardeners eh?

George: Uh-huh not ideal Jim, this cold weather's been playing havoc with my gooseberries.

Jim: Aye, mine too, mine too. In fact I think I'll have to pull them off and keep them in the airing cupboard.

George: Aye, well I think I'll let mine brave it out for a while . . .

Jim: Right then George, Arctic conditions, ground frost, freezing winds - what should all keen gardeners be doing at this time of the year?

George: Sitting in front of the telly with a wee dram in their hand.

Jim: I couldn't agree more George any particular brand of dram you recommend?

George: *(producing a glass of scotch)* Well here's my particular favourite for this time of year Jim, Grousellairis Scotchpissieyed.

George hands the glass of scotch to Jim who treats it like a potted plant.

Jim: Oh it's a healthy looking specimen George, the right colour, the right texture and . . . *(sniffs it)* that delicate aroma - do you mind if I take a cutting?

George: *(hesitating)* Aye, alright, but only a small one from the top mind.

Jim takes rather a large swig. George immediately reacts and pulls Jim's arm down.

George: I said from the top not from the bottom!

Jim: *(savouring it)* Mmmmmmmm, it's in a healthy nick is that one, George . . . *(holding it up to the light)* . . . it's er . . . it's one of the miniature varieties isn't it?

George: Well, it is now but it was a large one before you got hold of it.

Jim: You know a lot of viewers don't seem to get theirs to taste like this, and there's only one reason for that - isn't there George?

George: Och it's obvious Jim, they must be overwatering it.

Jim: And that's wrong isn't it?

George: Wrong? It's a bloody crime! *(he takes the glass from Jim).*

George: All they need is a gentle swirl like this . . . *(he swirls it)* . . . and then plant it straight down . . . *(he drinks it off).*

Jim: Of course George, to be on the safe side you've got to space them out well.

George produces a tray with a dozen glasses of scotch neatly spaced out on it.

George: That's right Jim, in this weather they want spacing out every two minutes.

Jim: For how long?

George: Oh until you're flat out on the bed.

Jim: Now surely, George, with such an abundance like this, then wind must be a major problem?

George: Oh it is, it is . . . but after this many I always go for the salts.

Jim: What kind of salts?

George: Somersaults usually. And of course wintersalts in the winter.

Jim: *(producing a letter)* Now then George, it's all been very interesting and finally we've had a letter from the viewer.

George: It was very nice of him to write.

Jim: Asking what's the best tool to use for cutting a privet hedge?

George: Er, shears.

Jim: Exactly George, cheers . . .

George & Jim: Cheers.

They touch glasses and drink.

The Seance

by Andy Hamilton

Willie: Rikki Fulton
Medium: Claire Nielson
Doris: Jan Wilson

In a dimly lit room several people are sitting round a table.

Medium: Is there anybody at this seance who wishes to contact someone who is . . . 'No longer with us'?

Doris: Er, yes, I'd like to contact my husband . . . William McAllister. He's about five foot four with brown hair and skin trouble.

Medium: Can we all join hands please, as I attempt to summon the spirit world.

They all join hands. The Medium closes her eyes and looks heavenwards.

. . . are you there, William McAllister . . . Are you there William McAllister?

Doris: *(irritated)* Answer the woman, Willie!

Medium: Sssssh! Please.

Doris: Well, it's just he never comes when you call him, if you know what I mean. Here, let me try . . . Are you there, Willie McAllister?

Willie: *(an echoing weary voice)* Oh what is it now, Doris?

Doris: Where have you been? You're late.

Willie: Of course I'm late, I'm dead aren't I? Now what is it you want, Doris, only make it quick, we're having a party here.

Doris: You have parties? In limbo?

Willie: Why not? There's sod all else to do.

Doris: *(falsely tender)* Now listen Willie, dearest departed darling. Do you remember when you were lying close to death, your life draining from you by the second? Well, Willie, there was something you forgot.

Willie: Oh heck, it wasn't our anniversary, was it?

Doris: No, Willie, you forgot to tell me where you'd put that £15,000 you'd taken out of your bank account the day before.

Willie laughs smugly.

Doris: Where's the money you old scrooge?

Medium: Please, please, Mrs. McAllister, let's not vulgarise the tone of the seance. Willie, have you any messages for us from the other side?

Willie: Hang on, I'll check.

Voices are heard in the background as he consults with fellow spirits.

Willie: Sandy McIlwham says to tell his wife Deirdre that he thinks he left the gas on.

Medium: But . . . Mrs. McIlwham died in an explosion this morning.

Willie: It's alright Sammy, you can tell her yourself. She'll be here in a minute.

Doris: *(wheedling again)* Willie dear, about the money.

Willie: Oh, shut your face.

Doris: What did you say!

Willie: I said put a sock in it you old nag-bag.

Doris: Willie McAllister . . . just you wait till I . . .

Willie: Yes, Doris? For years I let you push me around, well now I don't have to stand for it any more, see. I can give you some back now.

Doris: I don't know why you're so bitter, Willie. I mean, we had some good times, didn't we?

Willie: True Doris, for twenty years I was deliriously happy.

Doris: *(touched)* Ah Willie.

Willie: Then I met you. Ha, ha, ha. Walked straight into that one, didn't you Doris?

Doris: *(angrily)* I was a good wife to you, Willie. Faithful and hard working.

Willie: Hard working? Don't make me laugh. I wouldn't say you were lazy, but the last time you went to the zoo, you gave a sloth an identity crisis.

He laughs, and is joined by a female giggle.

Doris: Who's that with you, Willie?

Willie: Just another heavenly body, dear. I told you, we're having a party.

Doris: I expect it's that brazen little hitch-hiker they found with you in the car. No wonder you didn't notice the bridge was raised.

Willie: *(taunting her)* Nag-bag, nag-bag.

Doris: You'll regret this Willie.

Medium: For goodness sake Mr. McAllister, act your age. Please, for everyone's peace of mind, you may as well tell Mrs. McAllister where you put the money.

Doris: Right Willie, after all, you know what they say . . .'you can't take it with you.'

Willie: That's true Doris, they do say that . . . but then . . . *(he chuckles)* Who do you think is throwing all the parties up here?

Doris exits, fuming.

The Gallowgate Gourmet

by Bob Black

The Gallowgate Gourmet: Rikki Fulton

Well, hullawrerr food lovers and welcome once again to the Gallowgate Gourmet!

Now, as I'm sure you all know, the latest craze in the country is health food. It's flushin' through the country like a bad curry. So tonight, I'm going to do you a vegetarian dish which if it doesnae make yir mooth watter, it'll certainly make yir eyes watter. It's BEAN HOTPOT. Whit it'll be when Ah've finished wi' it, God only knows. Oh and just a word of advice to those people who can't bear tae eat the flesh of a living creature. KILL THE BLOODY THING FIRST!

And so to tonight's recipe, BEAN HOTPOT. Now it's a very popular vegetable - the bean. Very popular. In fact, whenever I'm on one of my lecture tours and mention BEANS, a loud ripple always runs right through the audience.

So, we begin with a bed of rice. *(pours rice)* Ach, let's make it a double bed. *(empties the rice bag)* To this we add our vegetables - and as always, these should be thoroughly cleaned. I use Fairy Liquid masel - 'cos it always keeps ma hands nice and soft. *(pours in the vegetables).* Ah can see some o' ye slaverin' already.

Now the cabbage has been pickled and drained through a pair o' old underpants. As a matter of fact, last night I was pickled masel and drained through . . . but that's another story!

Now we add the peppers. Green peppers, red peppers and we might as well stick in the Sunday papers. And then, of course, the beans. As always, hygiene is of paramount importance, so mind ye don't slash yir wrist on the can and bleed a' ower the recipe or it might turn intae a black puddin'.

And now it's time for a leek! I had one up against the wall just a minute ago. Ah, here we are. And, finally, the blue cheese - just tae gie it a touch o' that Guinness-say-kwa!

He opens the cupboard then staggers back from the smell.

Anybody got a gas mask?

He pulls out a drawer and takes out the cheese and plasters it over the contents of the bowl.

Aye, that's better. Now this has tae go intae the oven for six hours, or at least until the sanitary inspector's went home.

As you can see, the Gallowgate Gourmet kitchen has all the latest technological appliances, like this microwave oven. I'll just light it. *(he strikes a match)* I'll just . . . don't understand that, it doesnae seem tae light.

An R.A.F. officer in flying gear walks by.

Oh, I see whit it is. The pilot's went oot. Anyway, fortunately, I have another one here that I cooked earlier. There we are, absolutely perfect.

Using the old underpants he brings a casserole of smoking cinders out of the oven.

I must say this BEAN HOTPOT is especially good for those of you on a diet. Wan mouthfu' o' this an' ye'll be aff yir chuck fur a fortnight. Also I should tell you - it is a particularly handy dish anytime you feel like a good blow out.

So, there you are. Next week, I'll be telling you about seafood. I'll have advice for ladies worried about the size of their mussels. Men worried about the size of their winkles, and I'll also be showing you how tae crab a crab, peel an eel and wallop a scallop.
Aw ra best now.

Stable Companions

by Rikki Fulton

Man: Rikki Fulton
Woman: Claire Nielson
Conductor: Gregor Fisher

The conductor and a passenger arrive at the door of a sleeping berth in the corridor of a train. The man is wearing a long rain coat, a bowler hat and gloves and he is carrying an umbrella.

Conductor: Here we are sir. This is you. No.24.

The conductor opens the door and finds a gorgeous young dolly bird lying on the top bunk.

Man: Oh dear!

Conductor: Ah! Sorry Miss, but are you sure you're in the right berth?

Girl: Oh, I think so. No.24, isn't it? There's my reservation.

The conductor inspects her ticket.

Conductor: Er . . . Yes, seems right enough. Sorry, sir. Can't think how this could have happened.

Man: Oh, don't worry. Please. I'll be glad to take another berth.

Conductor: Well, that's just it. I'm sorry, but there isn't another spare berth on the train. We're chokka-block. It's either this or spend the night in the gents.

Man: What! You're not suggesting that I share with this . . . I mean, I'm a happily married man. What would my wife say?

Conductor: Well, nothing, if she doesn't know. And I wont tell her. *(he winks).*

Girl: I won't tell either - if you'd rather.

Man: *(very confused)* Well, I don't know . . .

Conductor: Come on. It'll be alright. What can happen in here. Blimey, there isn't enough room to swing a cat.

Man: It wasn't a cat I was thinking of . . . Oh, very well, if you're sure it'll be alright.

Conductor: That's the spirit! I'll waken you in the morning with a nice cuppa tea . . . and don't worry . . . I'll give the door a good knock before I come in. Goodnight then and happy dreams.

The conductor exits.

The man is embarrassed for a moment and doesn't know what to do. The girl lies on the upper bunk moving her body suggestively and making a play with her eyes. The man then proceeds to undress underneath his raincoat. He takes off his tie and his shirt and pulls them out at the neck. When he gets his trousers off, having done the necessary through the pockets of his raincoat, he very carefully folds them and then throws them under the bottom bunk.
When he finally takes off his raincoat he is quite properly dressed in his pyjamas still wearing his bowler and gloves. He ponders for a moment then puts his hat upside down under the bunk and gets into bed.

After a few minutes of silence.

Girl: Er - excuse me.

The man sits up startled and bumps his head.

Man: Er - yes, what is it?

Girl: I'm sorry to trouble you, but I'm awfully thirsty. D'you think you could get me a glass of water?

Man: Er - yes, of course.

He gets out of his bunk, gets her a glass of water, gives it to her and is about to get back into bed when she hands him the empty glass. He puts it back at the basin and gets into bed.

Girl: Er excuse me.

Man: Yes?

Girl: I'm sorry to trouble you again, but I'm finding it very warm in here. I wonder if you'd mind opening the window.

Man: Not at all.

He gets up. Opens the window, and gets back into bed.

Girl: Er - excuse me.

Man: *(with a sigh)* Yes?

Girl: I'm - er - finding it a bit chilly now - I'm sorry - do you think you could shut the window again.

Man: Do you know something?

Girl: *(coyly)* What?

Man: I've got a wee idea - I might be wrong - but I think you'd like to pretend that we were married!

Girl: Oh . . . well . . . Yes . . . I wouldn't mind!

Man: Right. Get up and shut the bloody window yourself!

Last Call

by Rikki Fulton

Rev. David Goodchild: Rikki Fulton
Floor Manager: David Hayman
Producer: John Bett

The Floor Manager is arranging a vase, a water carafe, a tumbler, bible etc. on a desk in the Last Call set.
Looking furtively in all directions he produces a bottle of gin and takes a swig.
Hearing someone approaching, he up-ends the bottle in the water carafe and stands in front, shielding it as the producer walks past.

Producer: Alright, Alex?

F.M.: Er . . . yes, Gordon. All set.

Producer: O.K. Fine. This'll be a take. Get the old buzzard in.

The producer walks out of shot. The Floor Manager takes the now empty gin bottle out of the carafe and stuffs it back in his pocket as the minister approaches.

F.M.: Alright, Reverend? Just sit there. O.K.? This is your first time, isn't it?

Rev. Goodchild: Yes. I hope it'll be all right.

F.M.; It'll be great, don't worry. Relax and wait for my signal.

The Floor Manager goes out of shot. The minister clears his throat nervously, then pours himself a glass of water and drains the glass. His eyes widen in mild surprise as the gin hits his stomach. He braces himself and waits to begin.
The Floor Manager gives him a signal and the Last Call music begins.

Rev. Goodchild: Good evening. Each night this week I shall have the pleasure of coming into your homes and chatting to you about normal everyday things. *(he burps)* Excuse me - things which, as we know only too well, sometimes turn out to be anything but normal, *(another rift blows his cheeks out)* and certainly don't happen every day.

He clears his throat and pours himself another glass of 'water'. He takes a mouthful and does a slight double-take of pleasant surprise.

I'm thinking, when I say that of 'The Good Samaritan'. Now - 'There was a Man' - if you'll pardon the John Cairney - who had no idea when he got up that morning that he was going to go down in history. As it happens he failed his Geography and Physics as well, but that's another story. You'll remember what Deuteronomy said to Leviticus about Exodus . . . er . . .

He can't remember so he takes another swig.

. . . so there's no point in bringing it up again. *(he burps)* Excuse me. Now, most of us, at one time or another, have had the opportunity . . . of being a Good Samaritan at one time or another without perhaps being . . . er . . . aware of it.

He pours another glassful and sips it.

Let me tell you about Jim and Elsie. That's not their real names, of course, but we'll call them Jim and Elsie in order to . . . er . . . . protect the innocent, Ha-ha . . . protect the . . . ha-ha . . . who loves ya baby! Now I first knew Jim . . .

He takes another drink and refills the glass.

(he starts to sing) It must be Jim . . . an ordinary guy . . .er . . . when I first knew Jim he was a happy-go-lucky devil-may-care . . . don't-give-a . . . for instance . . .

He takes another sip.

. . . and if he had a stiff with El . . . if he had a TIFF with Elsie . . . it's lovely water this - where dae ye get your water? Elsie would always say to Jim . . . Of course, that wasnae their real names . . . everybody knew their REAL names. It was wee Sammy Dunn and his wife Nirvanah, wasn't it. Nirvanah. Known as Nivir-Nivir for short. Nivir-nivir done talkin' . . . Nivir done borrowin' . . . Nivir let ye have a . . . Oh, we all KNEW her . . . I mean were ACQUAINTED with her.

Now pouring and supping continuously.

Anyway, Sammy began to change. Ah don't mean like Jekyll and Hyde . . . it was just . . . well, one day he'd be Sulky and Moody and the next he'd be Morecambe and Wise.

He takes another large swig.

And it soon became clear that he wis on the booze. Well, Ah tried tae do whit Ah could. So Ah got him tae get in touch wi' Alcoponics Analogous . . . 'cos he wis quite clearly an Archipelago . . . 's marvellous watter this . . . where dae ye go tae get this watter . . . listen . . . ha-ha . . . Ah think Ah'll get in touch wi' the Altiseptics Eponymous masel . . . TAE RESIGN. Anyway, this night Big Nirvanah an' me goes hame tae find Wee Sammy onny flerr absovery comblooteratit . . . an' the bath runnin' . . . Aye . . . watter runnin' doon the sterr - oot the close mooth . . . ye've never seen sae much watter . . . no as good as siss watter, mind ye . . . but watter everywhere . . . rushin' - pourin' - streamin' . . . Here, would you excuse me a minute . . . Ah feel a prayer comin' on. Ah'll be back in a minute . . . keep ma place.

He gets up and leaves the set.

Esscuse me, where's the lavvy? Could I have the privilege of using yir . . . esscuse me, sir, is there a lavvy in the house . . .

Dead Gallus!

by David Crooks and Bob Duncanson

Man: Rikki Fulton
Nurse: Claire Nielson
Corpse: Gregor Fisher

Inside a typical mortuary. Slabs, tables, shelves of chemicals, beakers and bottles, surgical instruments, etc. There are several corpses on trolleys and tables, covered head-to-toe with white sheets.
The covered 'corpse' nearest us, is a man (only slightly drunk, if even that. He should have slept it off by now). Waking up after a New Year party and thinking he's dead. He begins to moan, still covered by the sheet.

Man: Ohh . . . Ohh . . . *(becomes more musical)* Ohh . . . Danny Boy, the pipes, the pipes are calling . . . *(he calls out now)* Come on you lot, sing! Whit's wrang wi' ye? Are yiz in the huff or something?

He pulls the sheet off his face, but remains still otherwise.

Hello? Is anybody there? 'S dead quiet in here, intit? Where the hell am I anyway?

He takes a look round.

Oh I see, it's a mortuary. Oh well, I must be deid then.

He covers his face again. Then there is a pause, and he sits bolt upright. Shocked.

Eh! Deid! How come they picked on me? Could they no have got somebody wi' mair experience! Fancy that, eh? Wakin' up an' findin' oot yir deid! Bit o' a shock. eh? Kaput! An' I thought I was healthy an a'. I mean, I did the Glasgow Marathon - the whole twenty six pints an' three curries!

He shrugs.

Ach well. *(suddenly he has a thought)* Here, I wonder if I died intestate?

He raises the sheet and has a quick look down, then looks relieved.

Naw. Nae problem there. *(seems proud).* Fiona never complained anyway. Neither did the wife, come tae that.

He pauses, sighs, and takes a look round with idle curiosity. He sees the corpse next to him.

Oh, hello, son. I didnae see ye there. You snuffed it an a' eh? Must have been that cocktail. Irn Bru, Windolene and lighter fuel - some mixture that! Well, ye know what they say. Two's company, three's a shroud. *(laughs)* Gettit? Eh?

There is no answer. He shrugs again, bored.
Suddenly we hear a female voice calling out, sounding eerie from a distance.

Female: Hello? Is there anybody there?

The man stiffens. Shocked. Tense. Petrified.

Female: Is there anybody there?

Man: Aw naw! It must be a seance! Whit am I meant to dae now? I'm new to this game.

Female: Where are you?

Man: I'm here! I'm here! *(cups his hands round his mouth)* Receiving you loud and clear!

The swing doors open and a nurse comes in.

Nurse: Oh, there you are Thomson. We've been looking for you.

Man: Ye mean I'm no deid?

Nurse: Och no. You had a bit too much at the party and went for a wee lie down.

Man: Well, that's a relief.

Nurse: You'd better hurry up, Thomson, Matron's been looking for you.

Man: Aye, aye, just coming . . .

He goes towards the door, then turns and addresses the corpse that was beside him.

Well, it's been nice talkin' to ye. Hope ye have a good New Year when it comes . . . Any last request?

Corpse: *(rising up with an eerie voice)* Gonnae gie us anither o' thae cocktails?

The Seal Cull

by Guy Jenkin

Man: Rikki Fulton
Woman: Miriam Margolyes

A seaman is walking up a street with a kitbag on his shoulder. The harbour is in the background.

Voice Over: After a month grappling with the Arctic elements the seal cull is over and it's time to head home.

A woman is watching from her window. She sees him and her face lights up with joy.

Voice Over: Home to the joy of a warm fire and a woman's love.

She grabs her sealskin coat, pulls it on, and rushes down the hill to embrace him.

Voice Over: Home at last.

As she runs up to him, he coshes her over the head, pulls off her coat and stuffs it in his kit bag.

The Railway Ticket

by Quentin Reynolds

Clerk: Rikki Fulton
Customer: Gregor Fisher

At a B.R. ticket window a customer is waiting to be served.

Clerk: Yes?

Customer: A ticket to Edinburgh, please . . .

Clerk: Dae ye want a single, return, day return, weekly, monthly or season . . . Away Day, Student Rail Card, Senior citizen or H.M. Forces . . . First class, second class, facin' the engine, facin' away fae the engine, or facin' the toilets . . . smokin' non-smokin' or tryin' tae gie up smokin' . . . via Polmont or via Perth . . . Haymarket or Waverley . . . sleeper, non-sleeper, Big City Saver or Night Rider . . . restaurant car, buffet car or just a wee piece in yir haun . . . if yir takin' a push bike, motor bike, livestock or weans it's hauf the adult fare unless of course the adult is one of a party on a Family Rail Card . . . in any case you'll have tae wait until tomorrow because the last wan went five minutes ago . . .

Viva Espana

by Terry Ravenscroft

Bert: Rikki Fulton
Sybil: Margo Cunningham
Peter: David Hayman
Rose: Claire Nielson

A couple who have recently spent a holiday in Spain are intent on prolonging the joyful experience. Bullfight posters, Spanish guitars, matador's hats and swords adorn the sitting room wall along with wine carafes, Spanish lace dolls and other bric-a-brac.
Peter, dressed in a flamenco dancer's suit and hat, is sitting reading 'Teach Yourself Spanish'. On a coffee table are Spanish holiday brochures and a record player playing 'Rodrigues Guitar Concerto'. We hear the door chimes. Peter turns off the record player and breezes to the door to find Bert and Sybil. They are well wrapped up against the cold. Bert is wearing an overcoat, scarf and wellington boots. The coat is long enough to cover the tops of his boots. Sybil is wearing a fur coat. Peter is overjoyed at seeing them.

Peter: Bert! Sybil! Come on in out of the cold.

They step into the sitting room as Peter closes the door. They take in the decor and exchange puzzled looks.

Peter: Well, it's good to see you again.

Bert: It's nice of you to invite us, Peter.

Peter: *(just a little bashful)* Er . . . Pedro.

Bert: Pardon?

Peter: I'd rather you called me Pedro - if you don't mind.

Bert: *(giving him an odd look)* Oh. Alright . . . Pedro.

Sybil: Where's Rose?

Peter: She's in the kitchen preparing *la cena.* That's Spanish for 'the supper'. I'll give her a shout. *(shouts to the kitchen)* Rosita! Hey, Rosita! I know what'll bring her. Never fails, this.

He takes a guitar down from the wall and strums a few bars of flamenco music. Rose comes in from the kitchen dancing an animated flamenco. Bert and Sybil react with amazement. Rose dances round the room and Peter dances on the spot. He stops playing the guitar with a shout of 'Ole' and Rose grinds to a halt in front of Bert and Sybil. She curtsies, giving Bert an eyeful.

Rose: *(in a broad Glasgow accent) Buenas noches!*

Bert: And very nice, too.

Peter: Well, how do you like it, eh? We haven't seen each other since the holidays, have we?

Rose: Talking of which - guess where we went this year?

Bert: *(thinks for a moment)* Scarborough?

Peter: Spain, of course!

Rose: That's why I said *buenas noches.*

Bert: Oh, I thought you were bragging.

Peter: We've been talking Spanish quite a lot since we came back, haven't we, dear . . . *Donde?*

Rose: Where . . . *El Toro?*

Peter: The bull . . . Er . . . *Bano?*

Rose: The lavvy.

Bert: Remember that, Sybil, in case our bull ever gets caught short.

Peter: *(slighly embarrassed)* Bert - you don't think Rose and me . . . well, you don't think we're behaving silly, do you?

Bert: Silly? Nah - live and let live, I always say.

Sybil gives a knowing smile to Bert, who winks.

Sybil: And we know exactly how you feel, Pedro. Don't we Bert?

With a broad grin, Sybil whips off her coat. Underneath she is wearing a dress exactly the same as Rose's. Peter and Rose are delighted.

Peter: Well, well. I can see there's no point in asking where *you* went for your holidays. *(to Bert)* Did you enjoy it?

Bert: Enjoy what?

Peter: Why - Spain of course.

Bert: Oh, I didn't go. No - this year we took separate holidays.

Bert starts to take off his coat.

Peter: Well, where did you go then, Bert?

Bert whips open his coat, flasher style. Peter Boggles.

Bert: Sunnyview Nudist Camp!

Rose shrieks. Sybil smirks proudly.

Bonnie and Clyde

by Colin Bostock-Smith

Clyde: Rikki Fulton
Bonnie: Claire Nielson
Postmaster: Tony Roper

A doddering old postmaster is behind the counter in his post office. A geriatric couple enter dressed in gangster gear.

Clyde: Loak the door, hen, an' keep a lookout fur the cops.

Bonnie: Ah'll loak the door an' keep a lookout fur the cops . . .

Postmaster: Can Ah help ye?

Clyde: Aye, ye don't sell hearin' aid batteries, dae ye?

Postmaster: *(cupping a hand to his ear)* Whit?

Bonnie: Get oan wi' it! Tell him it's a stick up!

Clyde: *(raising his walking stick)* This is a stick up! *(he lowers his walking stick)* An' this is a stick doon . . . ha ha ha.

Postmaster: *(to Bonnie)* Whit's he wantin' . . . stamps?

Clyde: Do you know who we ur?

Postmaster: Furst class or second class?

Clyde: We ur . . . we ur . . . *(to Bonnie)* Who ur we again?

Bonnie: Ye wrote it doon oan yir bus pass!

Clyde: Aw, aye, so Ah did. *(to Postmaster)* Haud oan a minute, son . . . *(searches his pockets).*

Postmaster: Or is it a postal order ye want?

Bonnie: Ye can stoap huntin' . . . Ah've remembered! Bonnie an' Clyde, that's who we ur!

Postmaster: Ah'm gaun fur ma dinner in a minute . . . whit d'ye want?

Bonnie: We want . . . we want . . . *(to Clyde)* Whit *dae* we want?

Clyde: The pension?

Bonnie: *(to Postmaster)* This isnae Thursday, is it?

Postmaster: Ah don't think so . . .

Bonnie: Then it's no the pension . . . *(ponders)* Haud on, haud on, it's comin' back!

Clyde: *(eyes lighting up)* Ah always knew it would, sweetheart . . . *(he starts to undress).*

Bonnie: *(hitting him with her handbag)* No that, ye durty auld messin'! Ah mean, Ah've remembered whit we came in fur . . . we came tae rob the Post Office!

Clyde: Aw, aye . . . *(to Postmaster)* Where's the nearest Post Office son?

Bonnie: Yur staunin' in it, stupit!

Clyde: Aw, help ma God . . . an' me wi' ma new shoes oan . . . Ah never even noticed the dug . . .

Bonnie: Och, oot ma road! *(to Postmaster)* Right, you . . . hands up . . .

Clyde: . . . yur bum.

Postmaster: Hands up yur ain bum.

Bonnie: *(to Clyde)* Hands up *you* bum!

Clyde: Aw . . . *(to Postmaster)* Hands up, ma bum.

Bonnie: This is a hold-up!

Postmaster: Aw, is it? Where's yur stoakins then?

Bonnie: Whit?

Postmaster: Ye should huv stoakins ower yur heids . . .

Clyde: Naw, naw, we tried that . . . she hud a helluva boather wi' hur dentchurs. Tell him, hen . . .

Bonnie: Aye . . . Ah pullt the stoakin' ower ma heid . . . then Ah pit ma teeth in . . .

Clyde: Soon as she opened hur gub tae talk, hur wallies shot oot an' knocked a' the wee glass animals aff the mantlepiece.

Bonnie: Stoap tellin' him aw wur business! Look, ur you gonnae hand ower the money or no!

Postmaster: Ah'm warnin' you, hen . . . if you come any closer Ah'm no afraid tae have a go!

Clyde: Best o' luck, pal . . . Ah've been tryin' fur the last fifteen years . . .

Bonnie: Shut up an' get oan wi' it, Clyde . . . wur gonnae be late!

Clyde: Late fur whit?

Bonnie: Meals on Wheels . . . it's bananas an' custard the day!

Clyde: Right, that dis it! *(to Postmaster)* Get the dough intae this bag or Ah'll get hur tae climb through that wee windae an' indecently assault ye!

Postmaster: *(terrified)* Right . . . sure . . . certainly *(he starts shovelling money into the bag).*

Bonnie: Whit did ye say tae him, Clyde McCutcheon?

Clyde: Nothin', hen . . . nothin'.

Suddenly there are police sirens in the distance.

Bonnie: Hurry, the cops are comin'. Huv ye arranged fur the getaway vehicle tae pick us up ootside?

Clyde: Of course Ah huv!

Bonnie: Well, whit're we waitin' fur?

Clyde: Ah still cannae find ma bus pass!

Bonnie bops him with her bag.

Santa's Workshop

by John Byrne

Old Gnome: Rikki Fulton
Young Gnome: John Bett

There is Christmas music playing in the background as the old gnome works at his bench in Santa's workshop. The door opens and a young gnome comes in.

Old Gnome: Aw, thuv sent some help at last, huv they? Aw, great . . . jist great. When they saw the work's finished they go an' send a boy . . . Whit ur ye? Job creation scheme? Ah thought so . . . trust that auld skinflint tae get aw the handouts that are gaun.

Young Gnome: Who are you talkin' about?

Old Gnome: Santa bloody Claus, that's who . . . Well, whit ye staunin' aboot fur? Gie's a haun wi' these skateboards.

They sit screwing wheels on to boards while they talk.

Old Gnome: Look at ma hauns . . . fulla skelves. Used tae be Hula hoops . . . noo it's skateboards. Wance it wis Davy Crockett hats . . . that wis some year yon . . . Ah'm no kiddin' ye. Whit? An' thur wis ten o' us here at the time . . . still couldnae cope wi' the orders. Aye, wait till you're ma age, an' ye huv tae get up at four o'clock every mornin' fur tae feed them stupit lookin reindeers that pull the sledge. He's got a Jag an' a Bentley sittin' in the garage there an' he's still runnin' aboot wi' reindeer. Aw the weans think *he* makes aw this gear . . . they dae . . . Ah'm no kiddin'. We get letters aw the time . . . 'Dear Santa, could ye make us a go-kert . . . a fort . . . a cowboy set . . . a bionic wumman . . . a real wumman.' Honest tae God, it'd make ye greet, so it wid. An' it's no as if ye make good money either. Ye get paid in washers. Ah live in a wee toadstool up the road there . . . husnae even got an inside lavvy . . . Ah've been sweatin' ma guts oot here fur over two hundred years and auld Droopy Drawers has got aw the credit. He swanks aboot Lewis's in the rid pyjammies . . . 'Aw, aye hen, a doll's hoose an' a signed photie o' Tiger Tim . . . nae sweat.' Nae sweat! Aye no' fur him . . .

Young Gnome: Is there any chance o' meetin' the Boss? Ah mean, is he ever aboot?

Old Gnome: Ever aboot? Ye must be jokin' He's away in Majorca . . . He's got a villa ower there . . . Spends maist o' the year there. Jist comes up at Christmas tae pick up the bags o' toys . . . Boxin' Day he's aff again . . . Ah'm sometimes thinkin' o' jackin' it in, so Ah'm ur . . .

Young Gnome: Ah'm surprised you stuck it this long. You wouldnae find them puttin' up wi' this at British Leyland. In this modern society it could only be described as slave labour. Huv ye complained tae the shop steward?

Old Gnome: Shop steward! You mean the union?

Young Gnome: If I were you I'd get in touch - direct - wi' Norman Willis!

Old Gnome: Norman who? Oh, Norman Willis! Ye don't still believe in him, dae ye?

Unemployment

by Mick Deasy

First Man: Steven Pinder
Second Man: Gregor Fisher

Two men are standing in a bar. The first man produces a UB40 unemployment card. He taps it.

First Man: You know, I'm one of the three and a half million unemployed - I just hope the government knows what's going on.

Second Man: *(furtively producing a fistful of cards)* I'm twelve of the three and a half million unemployed and I just hope the government doesn't know what's going on.

The Driving Instructor

by Bob Black

Driving Instructor: Rikki Fulton
Manager: Tony Roper
Miss Buchanan: Claire Nielson

In a typical driving school office. There are some chairs, a desk, posters on the walls, 'Impact School of Motoring' . . . 'Pass with us' . . There is one door to the street and another to a back room. The manager is working at the desk.
The main door opens and a very old lady, Miss Buchanan, enters. Although she is old, she is very sprightly. A bit of an old devil in fact. She approaches the desk.

Manager: Ah, hello, Miss Buchanan. Ready for your driving lesson?

Miss Buchanan: Yes . . .

Manager: *(referring to his file)* Let's see, this will be number . . .

Miss Buchanan: Seventy nine! *(she giggles)* Tee hee! That was my age my last birthday.

Manager: Aw, that's lovely! I'll just get your instructor. *(he calls towards the other door)* Mister Jackson!

The door remains closed. He waits for a few seconds and then goes over and opens the door to reveal Mr. Jackson, the instructor, crouching, whimpering in a corner. He is a nervous wreck! He is terrified of going out in the car with her again. He is on the verge of breaking down completely.

Instructor: I can't go! I'm no ready!

The manager goes into the room and gets a hold of him.

Instructor: I don't want to go! I don't want to go!

Manager: *(dragging him into the main office)* Come on now, Miss

Buchanan's waiting. *(to Miss Buchanan)* What did you do on your last lesson?

Instructor: She showed me the other way to get out of a car!

Manager: *(puzzled)* The *other* way?

Instructor: Through the windscreen! *(shakes his head at Miss B.)* That was wan hell of an emergency stop. I skited alang the road like a human cannon-ball!

Manager: Didn't you have your seat belt on?

Instructor: *(he nods)* The seat went with me! *(he grows more emotional, sobbing and pleading)* I don't want to go! Don't make me go! She's a menace! We overtook a motorbike last week!

Manager: So!

Instructor: We were reversin' at the time! She goes everywhere at ninety miles an hour!

Manager: Well, you've got dual controls. Put your foot on the brake, man.

Instructor: That's with my foot on the brake! There's smoke and flames belchin' oot o' the tyres! Fire engines chase us for miles wi' their bells clanging! *(shakes his head)* They never catch us! *(growing more emotional)* The other day . . . the other day, she killed a wee dug. A poor wee defenceless puppy . . .

Miss Buchanan: Well, it shouldn't have been in the middle of the road.

Instructor: *We* were on the pavement! *(to the manager)* It ran up a close but she still got it! And I'm next . . .

Becoming hysterical, he grabs the managers lapels.

I don't want to go! I don't want to go!

He breaks down, slumping over the desk, absolutely exhausted.

I don't want to go!

Manager: *(sternly)* Mister Jackson! Pull yourself together! You've got to go! This school guarantees that every pupil will pass their test . . .

He looks at Miss B. She has taken a pair of gloves from her bag and is pulling them on with relish. Very flashy, leather driving gloves, with vents on the back. The man's conviction fades a little.

. . . eventually!

Turning to the instructor

You've got to go. You retire soon. You don't want to risk your pension.

Instructor: I don't want to risk my bloody life.

Manager: Come on now! That's it!

The instructor makes a great effort to calm himself. He stands straight, but is still tense and twitching.

Manager: That's better. Now, off you go. The car's outside.

Miss Buchanan: *(unaffected by all this and still keen and eager)* Which one's ours?

Instructor: *(drained, resigned and feeling doomed).* The usual. The one with the dents and the scratches and the roof torn off.

Miss Buchanan: *(disappointed)* Och, I don't like that one. The brakes squeal when I go round a corner.

Instructor: That's not the brakes. That's me!

They move towards the front door together.

Instructor: Now, listen. Tell her. We drive on the left hand side, okay? Even if all the nicest shop windows are on the right, *we* drive on the left!

Manager: *(to Miss B.)* I'm sure you've got that?

Miss Buchanan: Aye. I have. Come on then, Jacko! Let's burn rubber! Yippee!

She gives a skip and a jump and hurries out.

Manager: *(to the instructor)* And don't forget those hand signals!

The instructor looks at him pathetically, and nods. He crosses himself as if in silent prayer, then goes out after Miss Buchanan.

Nouveau Riche

by Laurie Rowley

Nouveau Riche: Rikki Fulton
Man: Tony Roper

A posh cocktail party. All the wets are standing around chatting. Nouveau Riche stands conspicuously alone. A man walks by and he stops him.

Nouveau Riche: You know, I just don't understand it. I'm a self-made millionaire. I've got a huge mansion near Edinburgh, four Rolls-Royce cars, a string of Arabian thoroughbreds, a yacht berthed in the Mediterranean and a private jet at my beck and call and yet for some unknown reason I'm still not accepted by society. Where am I going wrong?

Man: Well I . . .

Nouveau Riche: 'Scuse me . . .

He lifts his kilt and blows his nose on it.

Supercop: The Gate-crasher

by Colin Hudson

Supercop: Rikki Fulton
Drunk: Gregor Fisher

There is a noisy party in progress. Supercop knocks on the door which is opened by a drunk.

Supercop: Evening Sir.

Drunk: Officer?

Supercop: We have received information that you are running a disorderly house. Further, that your New Year party has been going on now for three days and nights non-stop. Also, you have naked women in there running amok and that you have had delivered from Johnson's Off Licence, fourteen crates of brown ale, thirteen boxes of assorted liqueurs, ten crates of whisky and six boxes of salt and vinegar crisps. Is that true?

Drunk: Perfectly true officer.

Supercop: Right then. *(he turns)* Okay lads, this is the place.

Four more traffic cops appear and they all join in the party.

POLICE

Supercop and a Long Lost Love

by Colin Bostock-Smith

Supercop: Rikki Fulton
Woman: Claire Nielson

Supercop has pulled a car in. He walks back from his motorbike to the car, which has a woman driver.

Supercop: Okay Stirling, oot o' the car. I made it eighty-six, what did . . . *(suddenly he recognises the driver)* . . . Oh my God!

Woman: Oh no! Andrew! Can it really be you?

Supercop: *(with much emotion)* . . . Maureen!

Woman: *(tenderly)* Andrew . . . how are you?

Supercop: I'm . . . I'm . . . *(with bitter memory)* I'm just the same as I was the day you left me at the church while you ran away with that big Jock McIntyre, the rotten dirty pig that he is!

Woman: Oh Andrew! What a fool I was!

Supercop: Aye, aye. Well, it's too late for regrets. It was your decision.

Woman: Don't be bitter, Andrew. I can see now, I made a mistake.

Supercop: Aye, and you made another one tonight. Eighty-six in a speed limit. Right, name - Mrs. Maureen McIntyre. Address?

Woman: Well . . . address . . . I really don't know . . .

Supercop: Ha! I suppose he's got you living in a caravan!

Woman: Not exactly. I just don't know whether to put our Edinburgh town house, or the estate in Argyllshire. Or perhaps the flat in Belgravia or the villa in Monte . . .

Supercop: *(with pity)* No fixed abode. And to think, if you'd married me, you could have had a cosy wee police house in Rutherglen!

Woman: Yes.

Supercop: But it was your decision. Now then, the car, your husband's, I suppose.

Woman: No, it's mine. He has two Jaguars, a Mercedes and a helicopter.

Supercop: Ah bet he hasnae got a motorbike!

Woman: No. No motorbike.

Supercop: Ha! Remember those rides we used to take, you on my pillion down the A74 in the rain?

Woman: I remember, we were so close. That's all in the past now. You must do your duty, Andrew.

Supercop: *(after a big mental struggle with himself)* Drive on! Drive on!

The car disappears into the distance. Supercop watches it go.

Supercop: *(sighing and shaking his head as he tears the page out of his notebook)* Och, the poor wee lassie. She's suffered enough already.

The Station Buffet

by Laurie Rowley

Man: Rikki Fulton
Assistant: Claire Nielson

Loudspeaker: The 8.10. train from Ardrossan has just arrived at Glasgow Central - seven hours late. British Rail regret any inconvenience to passengers.

The service counter in a B.R. station buffet. The counter is the kind you walk along to make your selection which is put on a plate by the assistant. The buffet is nearly deserted.
A man appears lugging two suitcases. He is exhausted after his train journey. He bangs on the counter for service.

Man: Come on, come on, let's have some service round here.

An assistant appears from a back room. She is surly and untidy.

Assistant: *(filing her nails)* Yes?

Man: What have you got for someone who's just spent nine hours on a train?

Assistant: Mutton chops, Toad in the Hole, or Mince.

Man: I'll have the mince, yes, definitely the mince.

Assistant: *(slopping the mince down onto the plate)* Boiled potatoes, chips or mash?

Man: Oh it's mash for me, yes, plenty of mash.

Assistant: *(slopping the mash onto the plate)* Peas, carrots or baked beans?

Man: Baked beans is perfect. Two helpings if you don't mind.

Assistant: *(piling on the baked beans)* Anything else?

Man: That's porridge there isn't it?

Assistant: Yeah.

Man: Slap us a couple of handfuls on will you . . . *(she does)*. . . and that rice pudding, some of that . . . oh and some of that thick custard.

His plate looks absolutely revolting.

Assistant: Anything else?

Man: No, that's fine . . . oh just a touch of tomato sauce. *(he pours it on himself and she passes him the plate)* That looks beautiful, just right. Thanks very much.

He has now reached the end of the counter. On the wall there is a poster of Jimmy Savile advertising British Rail. The man holds the plate in the palm of his hand and slaps the whole mess into Jimmy Savile's face. He picks up his cases and leaves with an air of immense satisfaction.

Un-Interrupted Coverage

by John Williams

Reporter: Dougie Donnelly
Man: Gregor Fisher

A man switches on the television set in his living room.

Reporter: . . . then at 2.45 Sportscene goes live to Parkhead for the New Year Celtic / Rangers game. This is the big one and it's *live* so make sure you get un-interrupted coverage of the match . . .

The man pulls on a Celtic tammy, sits back, and opens a can of beer.

Man: Don't you worry, Dougie, I will.

The man turns and we follow his gaze to his wife who is gagged and bound to a dining chair.

One Last Request

by Barry Bowes

Boss: Rikki Fulton
Secretary: Claire Nielson

The boss and his secretary are trapped in a lift for several hours. They are in a dazed and dishevelled state.

Boss: *(gasping)* We'll never get out of here alive, Miss Thompson!

He stares longingly at her.

. . . Miss Thompson . . . I've always wondered . . . what you'd say if I . . . took off your . . . May I?

He removes her glasses.

. . . I've wondered what would happen if I . . .

He reaches for her hair and a wig comes off.

You can't imagine . . . how I've felt . . . watching you move around the office . . . Those firm . . .

She clasps her hands to her breasts

Such superb body control . . .

She moves her hands quickly to her thighs.

Even after eighteen hours . . . Miss Thompson . . . Could you . . . could we . . . just once . . . before it's all over?

She consents willingly.

In the office corridor, a group of people are waiting outside the lift - cheering. The lift rises and opens, revealing the boss dressed in glasses, wig, bra and roll-on.

The Italian Restaurant

by John Byrne

Cyril McCluskey: Rikki Fulton
Bunty: Claire Nielson
Waiter: Tony Roper

Cyril McCluskey and Bunty, his date for the evening, are seated in an Italian restaurant. They are both elegantly dressed. He is urbane, arrogant and sophisticated (looking). She is adoring . . . a little coy. There is Italian music playing in the background.

Waiter: Ah signore . . . signorina. Menu?

Cyril: *(waving the menu aside)* No, no, no . . . I've told you . . . when you dine out with me, Bunty, you're dining out with a gourmand . . . a bon viveur . . . I mean, I've lived cheek to jowl with these people . . .

Bunty: Oh, Cyril . . .

Cyril: Fought at Monte Casino . . . swam bare-bottomed with them in the Po . . . what Cyril McCluskey doesn't know about Italian food could be inscribed on . . .

Waiter: A solitary strand of spaghetti, signore?

Cyril: Exactly, thank you.

Waiter: Prego.

Cyril: No, no. It's just the way she buttons her coat. Yes, we'll have some prego . . . *(to Bunty)* You sprinkle it on your moussaka, sweetheart.

Waiter: No, no . . . ees no moussaka, signore . . .

Cyril: Aw, that's a pity. Sorry, darling . . . moussaka's off . . . what else could I tempt you with? *(to waiter)* D'ye huv any them big roon' chewy things wi' the crust an' aw thon junk piled up in the middle?

Waiter: You want a pizza signore?

Cyril: Aye, Ah'll go fur wan in a minnit . . . after Ah've had wan o' them big roon' chewy things wi' the crust an' . . .

The Party Celebrity

by Donnie Kerr

Man: Rikki Fulton
Archie MacPherson: Himself

At a party in a hospital, various people are enjoying themselves. We see T.V. personality Archie MacPherson standing with a drink in his hand, chatting quietly to some people. A man appears in the background watching Archie closely, curiously. Waiting his chance. He approaches Archie, rather forcing himself on him, interrupting Archie's conversation as he grabs him by the arm. The man is eager, excited, over friendly and familiar. A bit of a 'Daft Punter'.

Man: It is you, intit?

Archie: Pardon?

Man: It is . . . *you!* Intit? See, me and the boys were just standin' over there like, and they said 'It's no him' and I said 'It is!' And they said it wouldnae be 'cos you wouldnae be here, and I said ye would! I said ye were probably visitin' someone in the Psychiatric Ward! Like the man who makes yir sports jackets.

Archie looks a little peeved. A little annoyed at having been interrupted.

Aye, so I bet them like, y'know. I bet them a tenner it wis you. And it is you. Intit?

Archie: *(modestly)* Yes, it is.

Man: *(delighted)* I knew it. You're my greatest fan. I never miss you on the telly. I watch you a' the time. Never miss a programme.

Archie: Well, thanks very much.

Archie makes to turn back to his friends, but the man grabs his arm again.

Man: I mean, my wife, well she cannae stand you. Ho! She thinks you're pure *rubbish!*

Archie looks crestfallen

But I says, 'no, no, fair's fair, he's no a' that bad . . .'

Archie: *(a little bit depressed)* Thanks a lot!

Man: So, eh, d'ye think I could have your autograph?

Archie: *(pleased now)* Certainly.

Man: *(searching himself, patting his pockets)* Have ye . . . eh . . . have ye got a pen?

Archie: I think so. *(takes a pen from his pocket).*

Man: And a bit of paper?

Archie: *(losing his patience a bit)* Yes . . . *(Archie takes a piece of paper out of his pocket).*

Man: *(a little embarrassed and self conscious)* It's not for me, of course, it's for my wee girl. Make it oot tae Alec!

Archie: Alec?

Man: Er, aye, we named her after me.

Archie finishes signing and hands the paper to the man. The man takes the pen too, but Archie checks him and pockets the pen himself.

Man: *(absolutely delighted-shaking hands)* Ho, ho! Well, thanks very much, ye know, for winnin' my bet, an' the tenner, and the autograph and . . .

He looks at the autograph and his face drops.

Whit? Oh.

He looks over to his pals and calls out.

Here, you win right enough boys. It wisnae Bamber Gascoigne at a' . . .

He crumples up the autograph and tosses it away, leaving Archie dumbfounded.

You Dancing?

by Barry Reeves

Teddy Boy: Rikki Fulton
Girl: Judith Sweeney

A crowd of people are chatting, drinking and dancing at a party. An ageing teddy boy approaches a girl who is seated. He is very cool.

Teddy Boy: *(combing his hair)* You dancing?

Girl: You asking?

Teddy Boy: I'm asking.

The girl stands up and the teddy boy takes her seat.

Teddy Boy: Thank God! My feet are killing me . . .

The Office Party Vamp

by Quentin Reynolds

Accountant: Rikki Fulton
Vamp: Claire Nielson

The office party is in full swing. The departmental 'Vamp' is trying to chat up a middle aged accountant. Both have drinks in their hands.

Vamp: What would you say if I told you I was wearing a lacey *black* brassiere . . . ?

The accountant's mouth falls open with excitement.

. . . a *black* suspender belt . . .

The accountant catches his breath at the thought of it.

. . . and tiny, *black, black,* panties . . . ?

The accountant's hand is shaking with excitement, so much so, that the ice cubes are steaming in his glass.

. . . there's no one in the kitchen. What do you suggest?

Accountant: We could go into the kitchen . . .

Vamp: *(gradually getting more and more excited)* Yes, yes.

Accountant: We could take off your black brassiere . . .

Vamp: Oh yes, yes.

Accountant: . . .and black suspender belt . . . *(he swallows with excitement)* . . . and tiny, black, black panties.

Vamp: Hurry, please hurry.

Accountant: . . . and wash them all in biological Ariel.

The Hospital Visitor

by Rikki Fulton

Visitor: Rikki Fulton
Willie: Extra

In a hospital ward. A man is in bed - very much bandaged, with his leg in a sling. A visitor arrives.

Visitor: Well, well - there ye are, Willie. So this is where yir hingin' oot, eh? Ah jist thought Ah'd gie ye a cry in in the bye-gaun tae kinna cheer ye up like. *(hangs his hat on Willie's leg).* Aye, Ah wis jist sayin' tae the wife there - Ah'd better away in an' see Willie afore it's too late. Aye, here yir no lookin' awfy weel - no weel at a'. D'ye think ye've ony chance?

Willie groans weakly.

Is that a fact? And whit does the docter say? Does he still come in tae see ye? Uh huh. ye'd wonder at him spendin' the time. Here Ah must say this is a nice wee place ye've got here. Is it let fur August? We're thinkin' on goin' abroad this year. Tae England. Aye, Ah fancy this place called Billingsgate. They tell me the fishin's awfy good.

Whit aboot yersel, Willie? Whaur dae ye fancy this year? Oh, ho, ho, ho - listen tae me. You've HUD yir holidays. Aw here Ah nearly forgot, the wife tellt me tae bring ye in some black grapes. But Goad, they're that expensive. Terrible expensive. So here - there's hauf-a-pun o' blackcurrants instead.

Whit's the food like here, Willie? No that they'll be givin' you much of course. Ah mean, they'll no be wantin' tae waste any. *(he lifts the blackcurrants).* Oh, by the way, Willie, Ah've got marvellous news fur ye. Marvellous news. Oh, this'll make yir day. Ah had a wee word wi' the docter afore Ah came in - and guess what? He says ye'll never work again. Is that no great, eh? *(he start eating the blackcurrants).*

Remember Big Sammy McIlwham? Mind, a dour big fella - sneaky like - used tae sing in the choir. He's deid! Aye, on the boolin' green last Setterday it wis. There he wis, folleyin' up a shot - an' he jist keeled ower - plonk in the middle o' the green. Oh the greenkeeper wis furious. Well, ye know the weight o' Big Sammy? Aye, it wis very sad. Very sad. Fur, ye

see, we were lyin' four up at the time.

He has a mouthful of seeds and wonders where to spit them. He eventually spits down in the direction of some concealed object. There is a PING!

Here, dae ye mind if Ah smoke ma pipe, Willie? It'll no bother ye, will it? Ye wouldnae like a wee suck yersel' eh? Naw, it'll take ye a' yir time tae keep breathin'.

He scrapes a match on Willie's leg, lights his pipe, and blows smoke in Willie's face.

Aye, aye, Willie. Things isnae good ootside either, ye know. Naw. Trouble in the Far East, trouble in the Middle East - even trouble doon at the East End the other night. An whit wi' hydrogen bombs an' radiation an' pollution - ye'll be faur better awa' oot o' it.

Aw listen, is the smoke botherin' ye? Here Ah'll open this windae. It's blawin' a gale ootside, but it'll keep the place fresh. No that Ah want ye tae catch yir death o' cauld. Oh, haw, haw, haw. Did ye hear that, Willie? Yir death o' cauld! As if you had time fur a cauld tae develop. Oh, here, Ah near furgot - there's some magazines fur ye. Ye can aye look at the pictures. Tho' Ah widnae start ony serials if Ah wis you.

Oh, an' that's another thing - ye ken Sandy McCulloch, well he's jist sterted in business for himsel' - Aye, as an undertaker. Ah said Ah wis comin' up tae see ye, an' Ah'd pit in a word fur him. Oh, he's got a marvellous hearse there, Willie. Oh, a beautiful hearse. He gied me a lift in it the other day. Ah wis sittin' beside him ye know, an' Ah said, 'My, Sandy,' Ah said, 'This caur's got a beautiful engine, ye can hardly hear it.' He says, 'Oh Aye,' he says, 'An' when yir ridin' in the back' he says, 'ye cannae hear anything at a '.'

Aye, well here, Ah'd better be gettin' on ma way. It's been nice tae see ye Willie. Aye does ye good tae hae a cheery word wi' an auld freen, eh? Ah'll maybe see ye again. Widnae bank on it, though. Well, cheerio then, Willie - an' don't forget - KEEP YIR PECKER UP.

Charles Dickens Birthplace

by Terry Ravenscroft

Baxter: Rikki Fulton
Elmer: Gregor Fisher
Willie: Finlay Welsh

In the living room of a council house, the furniture is old and battered. Against the wall is a hard-backed chair with the stuffing hanging out of the seat. Next to it is a vacuum cleaner. A thick rope separates the furniture from the front door area.
The owner of the house, Baxter, in shirtsleeves and braces, unshaven and bleary-eyed, sits at the table eating bacon and eggs. On the table is a stuffed cat and a transistor radio.
There is a knock at the door. Baxter rises and opens the door to a typical-looking American tourist who is carrying a newspaper.

Baxter: Yes, sir?

Elmer: Hi there. According to an advertisement in this newspaper this house is the birthplace of Charles Dickens.

Baxter: It is. Would you like a conducted tour?

Elmer: Say, that would be swell.

Baxter: I'll show you round then.

Baxter holds out his hand.

It's fifty pee.

Elmer takes out a bulging wallet and opens it.

Elmer: Sure. Do you have any change?

Baxter: *(looking hungrily at the wallet)* No, but there's £2.50 VAT as well. That makes it £4.00 all together.

Elmer: Oh, here you are then. You know, I always understood that Charles Dickens was born in England.

Baxter: No, it was here in the Castlemilk Estate. That's what inspired him to write *Bleak House.*

Elmer: *(looking round the room in awe)* So this is it then. The place where *the* Charles Dickens actually lived.

Baxter: Yes. *(he looks around)* Everything just as he left it.

He notices the unfinished bacon and eggs and explains it away.

As you can see, he was halfway through his breakfast when he snuffed it.

Elmer: And all the quaint furniture. Are all the pieces genuine Charles Dickens?

Baxter: Every last one of them. *(pointing to each in turn)* Over there we have Charles Dickens favourite settee. Here we have Charles Dickens sideboard. That's Charles Dickens yardbrush. Charles Dickens cat. The Charles Dickens transistor radio . . . And there on the bookshelf are his original works - his *Oliver Twist,* his *David Copperfield.*

Elmer: *(cutting in)* Have you got his *Little Dorritt*?

Baxter: No, just his books.

Elmer: *(soaking in the atmosphere)* My, my. And it was right here that he penned his immortal works?

Baxter: In this very room. *(he points to the hard-backed chair)* That's his writing chair over there. Next to his Hoover.

Elmer: Could I sit on it?

Baxter: On his Hoover?

Elmer: Could I sit on his writing chair?

Baxter: Oh. I don't see why not. Be careful you don't damage it.

Elmer: No, of course not.

Baxter takes down the rope and Elmer lowers himself reverently onto

the chair.

Elmer: Say! How about that!

Baxter: It was on that very chair that he wrote one of his great classics after coming home from the factory one night and observing in the street outside a small trouserless urchin.

Elmer: Which book was that?

Baxter: *Knicker-less Nickleby.*

Elmer: Say - this chair. Is it for sale?

Baxter: For sale?

Elmer: Yes, I'd like to buy it from you.

Baxter: You want me to sell you Charles Dickens writing chair? Sell you one of the country's most prized possessions? A part of Britain's heritage? No way Mister. No way.

Elmer: I'll give you ten pounds for it.

Baxter: Will you be taking it with you or shall I send it on?

Elmer: Here's your ten pounds.

Baxter picks up the chair, inverts it, and hands it to Elmer. Suddenly he notices something on the underside of the seat.

Baxter: Well, will you look at that!

Elmer: What's the matter?

Baxter: It isn't Charles Dickens chair after all.

Elmer: It isn't?

Baxter: No, it's somebody else's. There's his name, see - somebody called Chippendale.

Elmer: *(becoming very excited)* Chippendale? It's a Chippendale chair?

Baxter: And here's me thinking it was valuable. I suppose you'll be wanting your money back.

Elmer: No, no, I'll take it all the same.

Baxter: Well that's very good of you I'm sure, but while I don't mind selling you Charles Dickens chair, I couldn't possibly take ten pounds off you for the chair of an unknown writer like Chippendale.

Elmer: I'll increase my offer to fifty pounds.

Baxter: A hundred.

Elmer: Done.

Baxter: Yes, indeed.

Elmer counts out one hundred pounds to Baxter and Baxter hands the chair to Elmer.

Baxter: One Chippendale chair. *(he lifts the stuffed cat off the table)* And just so you won't be disappointed I'll throw in Charles Dickens cat as well.

Elmer: Why thanks. Goodbye then.

Baxter sees Elmer out then shouts to his assistant in the back room.

Baxter: Hey Willie - bring through another chair and a cat.

Willie appears with an identical chair and cat.

Last Call

by Rikki Fulton

Rev. I.M. Jolly: Rikki Fulton
(Minister of St. Bella's Parish Church, Glasgow).

Rev. Jolly: Hullo! 'And the wind rose. And Simon was much troubled. And they chided him saying, 'Why art thou so troubled with the wind?' And he was made to sit at the far end of the boat.'

'And it came to pass that he travelled for six days and six nights and came unto the house of Mary, but lo, she was not in. Whereupon he left a note unto her saying: 'I pulled thy bell and ye answered me not. I knocked thy knocker and ye answered me not. Wherefore I keeked through thy window and saw thee hiding under the bed. And I felt angry and betrayed. So I kicked thy ox and thy ass and all that was thine. And emptied thy dustbin over thy lawn.'

These are just two of the texts I'd like to talk to you about this Hogmanay. You know, the whole of our human existence is like one long Hogmanay. We set off along the road with hope in our hearts and bells ringing in our ears. A bevvy in one hand and a packet of crisps in the other. But, you see, we forget that we're all subject to the call - er - to the forces of nature! All these pressures - pleasures - have to be paid for. And if we eat only of the rich food and drink only of the red wine, what happens? We find ourselves throwing up down the toilet of life.
What you put into it, is truly what you get out of it!

The important thing to remember is that we can't be happy all the time. Look at me, for instance. I'm not always like this. Sometimes I'm quite miserable.

I used to visit an old lady. Let's call her Hilda. 'Cos that's her name. Hilda Harrison. Eighty-four, and a brighter, cheerier old dear you couldn't hope to meet in a month of Saturdays. She's Jewish! But she never lets anything get her down. Always smiling, always laughing, always ready with a cheery word. Makes ye sick! And she hadn't her troubles to find.

Her husband hadn't worked from the day they were married. Although,

to his credit, he did go to night school to learn a trade, so he'd know what kind of job he was out of. I just don't know how they'd have lived if Hilda hadn't owned a chain of supermarkets.
Anyway, about twenty years ago, he left her and went off with another woman. Hilda wouldn't have minded, but it was the marriage guidance counsellor.

Then her own grandson got a job with the Railway Police. What a tragedy. They took him down to Central Station one very dark night and told him, 'Your job is to patrol from the booking office to that red light over there.' He was never seen again. The red light was on a train going to Cornwall!

Then, finally, there was her grand-daughter. I was asked to perform the marriage ceremony in October - and six months later, she had a baby boy. Can you imagine that? Nearly eight months premature!

Which brings me to my opening reference to Simon.
So many people in our society are made to sit at the far end of the boat. Here's a letter I have received from a Mr. Archibald McClumpha.

Dear Mr. Jolly,
I am twenty-seven years old, have been married four times, and I have thirteen children. I don't go out much.
Last month my wife left me, took all the children - but left her mother. I recently lost my job at the Golden Future Employment Agency, and had to pay them redundancy. Since then, the electricity and telephone have been cut off, and there's no food in the house. And to top it all - last night the budgie died without even saying goodbye. That was the last straw. I am desperate. Mr. Jolly - please help me. To be honest, if I had the money, I would take the bus to Erskine Bridge and jump off.'

Well, of course, I couldn't ignore such a heart-rending plea from this poor man. So I sent him his bus fare!

Goodnight.